Credit Hell

How to Dig Out of Debt

Howard S. Dvorkin

WILEY

John Wiley & Sons, Inc.

Published by John Wiley & Sons, Inc., Hoboken, New Jersey.
Published simultaneously in Canada.

A previous edition of this book, *Credit Hell: How to Dig Out of Debt*, was
published in 1985.

For general information on our other products and services or for technical
support, please contact our Customer Care Department within the United
States at (800) 762-2974, outside the United States at (317) 572-3993, or
fax (317) 572-4002.

Wiley also publishes its books in a variety of electronic formats. Some
content that appears in print may not be available in electronic books. For
more information about Wiley products, visit our web site at www.wiley.com.

ISBN 978-0-470-64162-0

Printed in the United States of America

10 9 8 7 6 5 4 3 2 1

Dedicated with love and respect to my mother,
Natalie Dvorkin, without whose teachings this
book and all the practical information in it would
not be written within these pages. She was my friend,
my teacher, my strength, my cheerleader, and my mentor.

Contents

Preface

Welcome to my revised edition of *Credit Hell: How to Dig Out of Debt*, a user friendly, easy-to-read guide to dealing with your debts when you are struggling to make ends meet. Follow the advice in this book if any of the problems on the following list apply to you:

- More than 15 percent of your monthly take-home pay goes toward your debts.

- You can only afford to pay the minimum due on your credit cards each month.

- You have reached your credit limit on some if not all of your credit cards.

- You are using credit card advances to help you get through the month.

- You have little or nothing in savings.

- You are late paying your debts because you don't have the money you need to pay them by their due dates or you can't afford to pay some of your creditors at all.

- Creditors have refused to give you credit because of all of the negative information in your credit record or creditors are only willing to give you credit with terms that are less favorable than what they give other consumers with more positive credit histories.

- Debt collectors are calling you about your debts.

- Some of your creditors are threatening you with lawsuits.

- You and your spouse or partner are fighting over money.

- You are constantly worried about money.

Credit Hell guides you through the get-out-of-debt process from assessing the state of your finances and developing a budget, to negotiating with your creditors, consolidating your debts, and rebuilding your finances after your money troubles are over. It also tells you how to deal with important debts like a mortgage, car loans, and any taxes you may owe to the IRS. *Credit Hell* also lets you know when filing for bankruptcy is your best option and provides you with an overview of the process. In addition, this book explains why having a good credit record and a high credit score is important, how to order your credit report from each of the three national credit-reporting agencies, and what you can do to improve your scores and correct problems in your credit records. In addition, *Credit Hell* educates you about important laws that can protect you when you are applying for credit, using credit, or if a debt collector is hounding you. Finally, this book provides information about resources you can turn to for additional information and help as well as a glossary of terms that you may encounter as you dig yourself out of debt and try to stay out of debt in the future.

Chapter ONE

Assessing the State of
Your Finances

*Ed and Shana are totally stressed out because they can't keep up
with their credit card payments. Their problems began after one
of their daughters became seriously ill and they had to use their
cards to help pay her medical bills. They knew that money
would be tight until they got the card balances paid off, but then
Shana's hours at work were reduced and, with less monthly income, they began to fall behind on their debts. Ed and Shana's
lives have become a struggle and they worry constantly, especially now that debt collectors are calling to demand that they
pay what they owe. They have never been in such a bad situation before and the stress it has generated is causing tension in
Ed and Shana's marriage. Ed has become withdrawn and depressed. Ed and Shana feel as though their lives are ruined.*

If you are living in Credit Hell like Ed and Shana, there is
a way out, but it will take hard work, self-discipline, and
some sacrifice. Furthermore, it won't happen overnight.
After all, if your financial troubles are the result of over
spending, they probably developed over a period of

1

months if not years, so it's naive to think that there are any quick fixes. Be assured, however, that if you follow the advice in *Credit Hell: How to Dig Out of Debt,* little by little over time, your finances will improve.

You don't have to be drowning in debt to benefit from this book. For example, if you can pay your bills but you can only afford to pay the minimum due on your credit cards, the advice in this book can help you get out of debt faster so that you will have more disposable income each month enabling you to build up your savings faster. That way, if you are hit by unexpected expenses like Ed and Shana were, you won't have to run up your credit cards to pay for them.

It All Begins with a Budget

The get-out-of-debt process starts with the development of a budget. Then you can use it to prepare a practical plan of action that will get you to where you want to be—living within your means. Although you may resist the idea of living on a budget, the truth is, it's an essential money management tool and it will be difficult, if not impossible for you to get out of debt without one.

To start, figure out how you spend your money now by tracking your spending for a month. For the next month, write down how much you spend and what you spend it on, including anything that you purchase with a credit card, a debit card, a check, or cash, as well as any bills that you pay online or have automatically debited from your account, the money you give to your children, and other miscellaneous expenditures. Also, save all of your ATM and other receipts. No expense is too small to record in your notebook because small expenses will eventually add up to big ones. For example, in a year's time the $0.75 cents you spend for a newspaper each weekday, the $4 you spend every morning on your way to work for a latte, and the $6 you spend each work day for lunch will add up to a whopping $2,580!!!! And what will you have to show for all of that money? Ask your spouse or partner to track his or her expenses for a month, too. Your budget will not work properly unless you understand how *all* of the money in your household is being spent.

 For the more technologically savvy individual, the Budget Tool, Created by Consolidated Credit Counseling Services, Inc., is a money management application that tracks your total expenses and creates a simple budget to control your personal finances. The Budget Tool application is available for both the iPhone and iTouch. It can be downloaded at the App Store by searching for the term "Budget Tool."

The process of tracking your spending will help you become aware of exactly what you do with your money each month. That is a good thing because if you are like many consumers, you may not give much thought to it. You spend a dollar here, five dollars there, and then as the end of the month draws near, you wonder why you don't have much money left. As a result, you may use your credit cards and get cash advances to make ends meet. You will find great budgeting worksheets, tools, and instructions at www.consolidatedcredit.org.

Tally Your Spending Totals

After you have tracked your spending for a month, sit down with your notebook, check register, ATM receipts, and any other spending records you may have and then use all of that information to fill in the blanks under the Current Payments heading on the Budgeting Worksheet in Appendix A of this book.

You will notice that the expenses on that worksheet are divided into three categories: fixed expenses, variable expenses, and periodic expenses. Fixed expenses are expenses that stay the same from month to month—your rent or mortgage payments, your car payments, and other loan payments, for example. Variable expenses are expenses that change from month to month—the amount of money you spend on clothes, entertainment, meals, dry cleaning, and so on. Periodic expenses are expenses that you do not pay each month. They may include your insurance payments, property taxes, and your child's school tuition, among other things. Although you don't have to pay periodic expenses every month, you should be saving for them on a monthly basis so that when they come due, you have the money you need to pay them. Therefore, for budgeting purposes, you need to translate each of your periodic expenses into monthly amounts. To do that, divide the annual amount for each periodic expense by 12 and then record that dollar figure on the appropriate line of your worksheet under the Current Payments heading.

When you record your monthly expenses on the worksheet, be sure to include any debt payments you *should* be making but may not able to make because of lack of money. If you don't account for these expenses on your budgeting worksheet, you will understate your total expenses and you won't have an accurate picture of how much it costs your family to live each month. This will defeat the purpose of this exercise.

If you don't have exact amounts for your income and expenses, you may have to estimate those numbers. In this situation, I suggest that you understate your income and overstate your expenses when you complete the worksheet.

Once you have recorded all of your expenses on the worksheet and have recorded totals for each category of expense on the appropriate lines of the worksheet, add them all up. The number you end up with represents the total amount of money you are currently spending each month.

Compare Your Total Monthly Income to Your Total Expenses

Next, record your total net monthly income on the worksheet under the Current Income heading. When you are coming up with that number, take into account the monthly take-home pay of everyone contributing to the household expenses, which is your gross income less all deductions, including taxes, and any other source of regular reliable income you may receive, including child support or alimony payments, government benefits such as Social Security benefits, veterans benefits, Supplemental Security Income (SSI) payments, and so on.

When you have all of your expense and income information recorded, subtract your total monthly spending from your total monthly income. If the number you end up with is positive, then your income is greater than your expenses, which is good news. However, if the number is negative, then you are spending more than you take in each month. That is bad news.

If the news is good: Expenses are lower than income. If your monthly spending is less than your monthly income, you've got a budget surplus, which is a good thing. However, you may have a surplus because you are only paying the minimum due on your credit cards each month or because you are not making monthly contributions to your savings account or retirement plan. If you are paying just the minimum due on your credit cards, begin using some of your monthly surplus to pay off your credit card debts (and any other high interest debt you may have) more quickly. Your goal should be to get rid of that debt as soon as you can because the longer you take, the more interest you will pay to your creditors. The more interest you pay, the more your credit purchases will cost you. You should also review your budget worksheet to pinpoint expenses you can reduce or even eliminate and identity things you can do to live more frugally. Then, apply whatever money you save to your credit card debts, starting with the highest interest debt first. Meanwhile, until you have your credit card debts paid off, try not to use those credit cards.

Ideally, your surplus (either before or after you cut or eliminate expenses in your budget) will be big enough that you can pay off your credit card debts and, at the same time, save money or increase the rate at which you are saving. Financial experts advise that you keep a minimum of six months of living expenses in a savings account as a financial safety net. Then, if you are hit with an unexpected expense—essential home repairs, medical bills, car repairs, or other expense—or if you or your spouse or partner lose your job, you can use those funds to help pay your family's living expenses and debts. Without that safety net, you may run up debt on your credit cards to help pay for things. Because of the very high interest you pay for credit card debt, this is not a desirable thing. Once you have a minimum of six months of living expenses in your savings account, continue to build your savings so that you will have the money you need to help fund your children's educations and your retirement, and to help pay for a new home, a new car, new furniture, a vacation, or something else that is important to you.

Tip

Financial experts advise that you allocate at least 10 percent of your monthly income to savings. If you can't afford to save that much right now, try to save at least 5 percent. The important thing is to begin saving something each month, even if you can only afford to save a small amount, so that saving becomes a financial habit. Over time, as your financial situation improves, you can increase the amount you are saving. However, contributing to savings comes with one caveat. If you have a lot of debt and that debt comes with high interest rates, it may be better to get the high interest debt paid off or significantly reduced at the expense of building up your savings.

If you can't afford to pay off your credit card debts faster and boost your savings at the same time, focus on paying off your credit card debts first. Once you pay off the credit card with the highest rate of interest, apply the money you were paying on that debt plus whatever else you can afford to paying off the credit card with the next highest interest rate, and so on. There is an exception to this advice, however. The exception applies if you think that your job (or your spouse or partner's job) may be in jeopardy. In that case, unless you already have enough in savings to cover six to nine months of expenses, concentrate on building up that account as quickly as you can, and then focus on paying off your credit card debts.

If the news is bad: Monthly expenses exceed your income. Since you are reading this book, I imagine that after comparing your monthly expenses and income most of you will discover that your expenses exceed your income. In other words, each month, you are probably making up the difference between your income and your expenses by using your credit cards, getting cash advances, by not paying some of your bills at all, and/or by doing without. As a result, you may be getting deeper and deeper into debt each month.

You should work toward achieving two goals when you have a monthly budget shortfall. Your first and most immediate goal should be to reduce your spending by enough that your monthly income will cover all of your monthly financial obligations—your family's living expenses and debts. Once you have achieved that goal, your next goal should be to reduce your spending even more so you can begin saving each month. Exhibit 1.1, Spending Guidelines, indicates how financial experts generally agree you should allocate your dollars. If your spending in any one of the expense categories exceeds what you are

Exhibit 1.1 Spending Guidelines

Expenses	Amount of Your Income (%)
Housing	25
Transportation	15
Utilities	10
Food	10
Clothing	5
Medical/Health	10
Personal	5
Entertainment	5
Other	5
Savings	10
Total	100

currently spending, you may need to focus on reducing your spending in that area. The section titled Tips for Reducing Your Spending, later in this chapter, provides specific advice for how to live on less.

If you are deeply in debt, you may not be able to work toward achieving both goals right away. If that's the case, focus first on reducing your spending so you can live on your income, and then later, as things improve, you can work toward the second goal.

It's also possible that you will have to increase your household income in order to achieve your first goal. That may require that you and your spouse or partner get second jobs, do freelance work, or even find better paying full-time positions. You may also want to consider asking your older children to work part time so that they can help

9

pay some of their own expenses, assuming that their school performance won't be jeopardized.

Make budget cutting a family affair. Share your budget worksheet with your entire family, including your children. Ask everyone for suggestions on how to reduce the family's spending and then each month review with them the progress the family has made reducing its spending. Involving your children in the process is a good way to teach them to be responsible money managers as adults.

Tip

Getting your children involved in your family's finances at an early age will lead to important benefits for them later in life when they are managing their own money. Don't be afraid to talk about money during your family meal times. Such conversations provide you with an opportunity to teach your children important life lessons that should pay substantial dividends throughout their lives.

Maria and Jorge just can't seem to make a dent in their credit card debts and they worry that they are spending so much money paying on those debts that they will never be able to save enough to buy a bigger home and to help their children go to college. As a result, Maria went to the library and found a book about budgeting and she and Jorge decided to put the book's information into action. Following the book's directions, they figured out where their money was going each month. They were surprised by what they learned. For example, Maria and Jorge found out that their weekday restaurant lunches were

10

costing them close to $300/month and that the monthly cost of Maria's daily latté amounted to $60. Those two expenses alone amounted to $4,320 each year—money that they could use to pay off their credit card debts.

After they identified expenses that they could reduce, Maria and Jorge met with their 12- and 16-year-old children. In their judgment, the children were old enough to become actively involved in helping manage their family's finances. Also, Maria and Jorge felt that involving them in discussions about money would help prepare their children to manage their own finances as adults. During the family meeting, Maria and Jorge shared their family's monthly expense and income information with their children, discussed why they wanted to pay off their credit card debts more quickly, and shared with them the things they intended to do to help achieve that goal. Maria and Jorge also asked their children for suggestions about things they could do to live on less. The 12-year-old offered to start babysitting in order to earn her own spending money and was excited about becoming more financially independent. The 16-year-old offered to get a weekend job to help pay for his own gas and car insurance. Maria said that she would post a copy of their family budget on the refrigerator and everyone agreed to meet at the end of each month to discuss how well they were doing meeting their financial goals. Everyone felt good about the challenges ahead and liked the idea that they were all pulling together.

The percentages in Exhibit 1.1 illustrate what proportion of your income financial experts say consumers should spend on each of the expense categories listed in

11

the exhibit. If you are spending a larger percentage of your income on any of the expense categories, then those are the expense categories you should target first for budget cuts. Bear in mind, however, that the percentages in this exhibit are spending guidelines, not rigid numbers. Therefore, you may need to allocate relatively more or less of your income to certain expenses. For example, if the cost of housing is particularly high in your area of the country, then spending 25 percent of your income on your mortgage or rent payments may be unrealistic, but at the same time your area may have a great public transportation system, so spending 15 percent of your income on that expense may be excessive. However, a high cost of living typically coincides with a higher than average income.

What Next?

If you can reduce your expenses by enough that you can pay all of your family's living expenses and debts out of your household's monthly income, fill out the blanks under the Revised Income column on the budgeting worksheet in Appendix A. These new dollar amounts represent how you intend to allocate your money each month to get rid of your credit card and other high interest debts and build up your savings as quickly as possible. In other words, you now have a household budget. Transfer the numbers onto the form in Appendix B, Your Household Budget. Make a copy of the form and post it in a prominent location like on your refrigerator door or on a mirror that you use every day so that you will be reminded to stick with it.

Make sure that everyone in your family who will be involved in making your budget work understands why your family needs to reduce its spending and live on a budget. Let them know that as your finances improve, it may be possible to add back into the budget some of the spending items that you had to cut, but not if it means running up your credit cards again. You may also want to explain what is at stake if your family does not change its financial habits. For example, your family may lose the car you financed or are leasing, the furniture you financed, and maybe even your home; or you may never have enough money to purchase a home or to help your children pay for college, or to send them to summer camp, and so on.

After you have lived with your budget for a month or two, compare your actual spending to what you budgeted. You may need to make some adjustments to your budget if certain expenses are always higher than what you budgeted. Before you do, however, be sure that you understand why the changes are necessary. Make sure that it is not because you or someone else in your family is not taking your budget seriously enough. If that's the case, get serious; don't adjust your budget.

Once you feel certain that you have a workable budget, review it at the end of each month. Over time, you may need to revise it if certain expenses go up or down— your medical insurance or your mortgage payment for example—if your household income increases or decreases as you pay off your debts. In other words, you should treat your budget as a work in progress that will change as your finances change.

It is possible that some of the expenses in your budget will increase or decrease according to the season. For example, your heating and cooling costs may be especially high or low during certain months of the year. You may need to make adjustments in other areas of your budget in response to the seasonal changes. However, some utility companies have payment plans that may improve your budget by allowing you to pay a set amount of money each month rather than having your utility bill fluctuate dramatically from season to season.

If You Can't Reduce Your Spending to Match Your Income

It is possible even after you have done everything you can to reduce your spending and increase your income, that your income will not be enough to cover your living expenses and debts. If that is the case, you must decide which debts and living expenses you will and won't pay until your financial situation improves. Meanwhile, you must decide what to do about your debts. Ideally, you can figure out a way to pay them—maybe by getting your creditors to lower your monthly payments—especially if assets that you do not want to lose to your creditors secure any of your debts. Your car loan and mortgage are examples of secured debts. Chapter 2 explains the difference between secured and unsecured debts, explains what to pay when you can't afford to pay everything, and lays out your options for dealing with your debts.

When you can't make ends meet, it's a good idea to sell your nonessential assets, especially if you own them outright, and apply the sale proceeds to your highest interest-bearing debts. If you have used any of the assets you sell as loan collateral, you must apply the sale proceeds from the sale of those assets to the loans they are securing. Examples of nonessential assets include extra vehicles, recreational vehicles, boat, motorcycles, furniture, and so on.

If you can't stop spending even though you know you should, you may have an emotional problem with money. Debtors Anonymous (DA) can help. The organization uses the techniques of Alcoholics Anonymous to help people overcome their spending addictions. You can find a DA chapter near you at www.debtorsanonymous .org or by calling (800) 421-2383.

Don't Make Matters Worse

Doing any of the things on the following list will make your financial situation worse when you are struggling to get out of debt:

- *Use your credit cards or get a cash advance.*

- *Write a check when you know you do not have the funds to cover it.* Not only will you have to pay bad check fees, but the creditor may sue you and you may face criminal prosecution. Also, the bad check will impede your ability to open future bank accounts with your current bank and other financial institutions.

- *Get a pay-day loan.* A pay-day loan is a very expensive source of quick cash. Here is how a pay-day loan works: You write a postdated personal check payable to the pay-day lender, which may be a check cashing company, a finance company, or some other business. The check will be for the amount you want to borrow plus a fee. The fee will either be a percentage of the check's face value or a set amount that is based on the amount of money you borrow (for example, for every $50 or $100 you borrow, you pay X amount of money to the lender). In turn, the lender will pay you the amount of the check minus the fee. At the end of the loan period—usually a couple of weeks—you will be obligated to repay the loan. However, if you cannot afford to, you can extend or roll-over the loan for another loan period, but you will have to pay an additional fee. Due to the costs associated with this type of financing pay-day loans should be a financing vehicle of last resort.

- *Get an advance-fee loan.* Advance-fee loans are scams, pure and simple. Firms that make these kinds of loans advertise that you will qualify for a loan regardless of the state of your finances and the condition of your credit history. However, you may have to pay a substantial amount of money just to apply for the loan and once you do, the lender may disappear, leaving you with less money and no loan. If you do get a loan from an advance-fee lender, the terms of the loan will be unattractive, cost you a lot more than if you had borrowed from a legitimate lender, and may get you deeper in debt.

- *Pawn your possessions.* A pawnshop loan is an expensive source of money. Not only will you have to leave the item you pawn at the pawnshop but also the pawnbroker will only lend you between 50 percent or 60 percent, or even less, of the item's resale value. You will have a couple of months to repay the loan and during this time, the pawnshop will charge you a very high rate of interest—between 10 percent and 20 percent a month—which translates to an annual interest rate of between 120 percent and 240 percent! Furthermore, if you can't afford to repay the loan, the pawnshop will keep the item you pawned and resell it.

Tips for Reducing Your Spending

Looking for things to cut in your budget? When you examine your budget worksheet, some expenses may jump right out as candidates for reduction or elimination, but if not, pay particular attention to your variable expenses since they usually represent nonessential expenses that are totally within your control. For example, you can decide to eat out less, make your child's school lunch each day, reduce what you spend on groceries, stop all recreational shopping, give up your monthly manicure, skip your daily latté or espresso, and so on. If you lack for budget-cutting ideas, review the ones in this section. Although some of the ideas may not work for you, they may trigger other cost-saving ideas that do.

Reduce Your Housing Costs

- Find a less expensive place to live if you are renting and you are close to the end of your lease.

- If your lease is not close to being up, consider subleasing your rental home or apartment, assuming your lease allows it. If it does not, ask your landlord about subleasing anyway. He or she may let you sublease your place if it means a continued steady stream of rental payments. Make sure to document such an arrangement in writing.

Warning

If you sublease the place you are renting to someone else, your name will still be on the lease even though someone else will be paying the rent. Therefore, depending on your state, if that other person misses any of his or her payments, you may be legally liable for them. You may also be liable for any damage the sublessor may do to the rental. If you want to sublease the place you are renting to someone, it's important that you choose someone who is honest and trustworthy and who you are confident will pay the rent on time.

- Get a roommate, assuming your lease allows roommates. If it does not, ask your landlord if you can have

18

a roommate. Be certain to mention pending financial hardships in order to convince the landlord to allow you to modify the lease.

- Move in with your family or with a friend until your financial situation improves.

- Sell your home and purchase something less expensive, assuming you can sell it for enough to pay the total balance due on your mortgage.

Warning

When you are shopping for a less expensive home, don't just consider how much your mortgage payments will be. Also take into account the cost of maintaining and repairing the home, insuring it, the average amount you will have to pay each month on utilities, applicable homeowner fees and real estate taxes. When you take these other costs into account, the home that appears to be less expensive than the one you own now based on how much your mortgage payments may turn out to be substantially more expensive when you take those other expenses into account.

- Keep your home, but rent it out and find a less expensive place to rent or buy. This option does not make sense unless the rent you receive for your home will cover your mortgage payments, taxes, and insurance, at a minimum. Also, availing yourself of this option exposes you to some risk if your tenant does not pay the rent or if your rental home remains empty for extended periods of time.

Cut Your Utility Costs

- Insulate your home, caulk your windows, and use weather stripping.

- Take advantage of the free energy audit your utility company may offer. The audit will pinpoint actions you can take to increase your home's energy efficiency. Many utilities offer rebates to customers who make their homes more energy efficient and also sponsor low interest loan programs to help pay for those improvements. If your utility company does not offer free energy audits, it may be able to refer you to a qualified energy professional who will conduct an audit for a reasonable fee.

- Buy energy efficient appliances. (Major appliances must have affixed to them an Energy Guide Label that provides potential buyers with information about their energy efficiency.) Your utility companies may subsidize some of the cost of upgrading your appliances to energy efficiency.

- Save money by enrolling in your utility's load management or off-rate program if available and applicable to you.

Reduce the Cost of Your Phone and Phone Service

- Get rid of your cell phone if you rarely use it or if you could get along without it. Having a cell phone is convenient, but in most cases, that's exactly what it is—a convenience, not a necessity. Another option, depending on how their costs compare, is to get rid of your home phone (land line) and use your cell phone as your primary phone.

- Many carriers now often offer bundling options for utilities like cable, telephone, and Internet that can save you money on your monthly bills. Check with your service provider to see what options are available in your area.

- Shop around for the best deal on cell phone service. If you find a better deal than the one you have now, ask your current service provider to beat it. It may be willing to since beating the other company's offer could be cheaper than trying to find a new customer to replace you if you switch providers. However, if you still want to switch service providers, wait until your current contract is up. Alternatively, find a provider that offers you a low rate for service that is comparable to or better than what you have now so that you will still save money if you switch, even though you will be legally obligated to continue paying for your current service until your contract is up.

- Make sure that your calling plans are appropriate given your usage patterns. For example, a flat rate or measured service plan might be practical given your usage patterns. You can usually obtain this information by calling your current service provider and asking them to analyze your usage.

- Take advantage of all of the free hours that come with your cell phone plan. Find out if unused minutes in one month can be rolled over to the next month.

- Check your local phone bill to see if you have optional services you don't really need or use—caller ID or call blocking, for example. Each option you drop could possibly save you hundreds of dollars annually.

- Make your long distance calls during the least expensive times of the day or week. Depending on your calling plan, evening and weekend calls may be considerably cheaper than calls made during the day and on weekdays.

- Dial your long distance calls directly. Using the operator to place a call can cost you an extra $1 to $3. Avoid using an operator for Directory Assistance as well. Also, watch the rates on calling cards when you call long distance. With some cards, you could end up paying double if not triple what a normal call would cost you.

Spend Less on Food and Entertainment

- Plan your meals a week at a time based on the amount of money you have budgeted for groceries each month and then try to purchase all of the groceries you will need for that week by making just one trip to the grocery store. The more trips you make, the more you are apt to spend.

- Buy in bulk when practical. However, be careful about purchasing perishable items that may go bad before you have a chance to consume them.

- Use coupons and take advantage of rebates and sales.

- On workdays, you and your spouse or partner should consider packing your own lunches rather than eating out. Also pack your children's lunches.

- Give up after-work happy hours or limit yourself to the number you go to and the number of drinks you buy.

- If you enjoy entertaining at home, make your dinner parties potluck affairs where everyone who's invited must bring something for the meal.

- Get rid of any premium cable and satellite channels you pay extra for—HBO and Showtime, for example.

- Borrow books, DVDs, and videotapes from the library rather than buying them, or exchange these items with friends who have tastes similar to yours.

Cut Back on Your Clothing Costs

- Don't shop for the fun of it or to pass the time away. Purchase only what you need. Spending money should not be a hobby!

- Buy on sale, at discount stores, and at resale shops.

- Shop at yard sales. If you shop in the right neighborhoods, you can get real bargains on high-quality items.

- Swap clothes with friends.

- Make certain that a "sale price" is really a bargain.

Reduce Your Transportation Expenses

- Use public transportation to get to and from work, or carpool when possible.

- Sell your second car if you can do without it.

- If your car is expensive to operate and maintain (consider costs of gas, insurance, and repairs), sell it and purchase a less expensive vehicle.

- If you need to replace your current vehicle, think about buying a used one. Find a reliable used car by educating yourself about which ones hold their value over time and have the best repair records. When you find one that you like, have the car checked out by a mechanic you trust—don't take the seller's word that the car runs well and is problem-free—especially if it is being sold "as is." Also, compare the seller's asking price to the car's *Kelley Blue Book* value by going to www.kbb.com or using a hard copy of the book at your local library. The *NADA Official Used Car Guide* is another good resource.

- If you want to buy a new car, research the best one to buy based on its purchase price, available financing, cost to insure, repair history, and gas mileage. You can find new car guides in your local library and bookstore or check out online resources like www.checkbook.org or www.autoweb.com. Also, call multiple car dealers, ask them for their best price and let them know you are calling other dealers.

 It's usually better to purchase a used car from someone you know and trust because compared to a used car salesperson, that person will probably be more forthcoming about any problems with the car and more inclined to charge you a fair price.

- Consider purchasing an extended warranty.
- Have your car serviced regularly so that it will be less apt to break down.

- Find a skilled, honest auto mechanic before you need one so that you don't end up paying too much for needless or inadequate repairs because you have to get your car repaired right away and don't have time to check out the mechanic you use. Look for a mechanic who is certified, well established, and has done good work for someone you know. Also, check out the mechanic's complaint record with your local Better Business Bureau.

Lower Your Insurance Costs

- Contact your insurance agent to discuss how you can reduce your insurance costs. Among other things, your agent may suggest raising the deductibles on the collision and comprehensive portion of your auto insurance or dropping that coverage entirely if your car is old. The agent may also suggest raising the deductibles on your health insurance policy or reducing the amount of insurance you have.

- Shop around for insurance. You are not wedded to any insurance company.

- Don't pay for insurance you do not need—appliance insurance, car rental insurance, flight insurance, credit life insurance, insurance on the lives of your children, and so on.

- If you have a whole life or universal life insurance policy, think about converting the policy to a term life policy. This kind of policy has low premiums and no cash value.

- Do an insurance check up every few years to determine if you have enough insurance or if you need different coverage. Over the years, your insurance needs are apt to change.

- You don't need life insurance if you have no dependents. Therefore, if you have a policy, cancel it.

- Take advantage of all the discounts you are entitled to. For example, you may be eligible for a discount on your auto insurance if you complete a state-sponsored driver's education class and for a discount on your homeowner's insurance if you install a security system in your home. Purchasing your auto and home insurance from the same company may qualify you for a discount too.

 Warning Life insurance is a bad investment. It is a very expensive way to save money. Don't believe anyone who tells you otherwise.

- While it can be difficult to afford health insurance these days, it can be risky, both financially and health-wise, to go without. In fact, just over half of Americans who file for bankruptcy list medical bills as a significant reason for filing. And putting off routine medical care may lead to more serious (and expensive) health problems down the road. Health insurance is one way to help pay for the care you need, and perhaps even keep your family out of bankruptcy.

- An estimated 43 million American families today, many of them middle class, are going without health insurance because of the rising cost. Even those who get health insurance through their employer may find they have to pay more out-of-pocket expenses.

While there's no easy solution to the health insurance dilemma, there are strategies you may be able to use to help make it more affordable. Here are places to start:

- *Shop frequently.* Web sites such as www.health insurancesearch.com, www.ehealthinsurance.com, or www.insweb.com can be good starting places. You should also talk with an experienced local insurance agent who is knowledgeable about programs in your local area. It can also be helpful to call your local Chamber of Commerce to find out if they have a health insurance committee that can provide information or referrals. And ask friends and relatives about their health insurance. They may be able to refer you to a company or insurance agent who can help you find a better plan.

- *Understand your coverage options.* You'll likely have the choice of major medical, HMOs, PPOs, or POS plans. It's important to pick one that fits with your budget and medical needs. Generally, the more flexibility you have in choosing doctors and facilities, the more you'll pay. Weigh the cost and benefit of those choices.

- *Don't go without.* Do what you can to avoid a gap in coverage, or you may lose the protection of the Health Insurance Portability and Accountability Act of 1996. HIPAA places limits on the ability of health insurance

27

companies to exclude pre-existing medical conditions. To be eligible, you must have been part of a *group* insurance plan and meet other requirements to qualify.

- *Short-term policy.* Even if you can't go from one group policy to another, a short-term individual policy may be helpful to keep up with any unexpected medical expenses. If necessary, look into a short-term medical policy until you start another job or can find other insurance. You may not get the best coverage, but it may be better than no coverage at all.

- *Consider COBRA.* Generally, if you're employed at a company with 20 or more workers and you leave your job, have your hours reduced (making you ineligible for employer-paid insurance), are terminated other than for gross misconduct, or get divorced and lose coverage under your spouse's plan, you can likely elect to continue your insurance coverage under COBRA. You'll have to pay the full amount of the premium plus an administrative fee of 2 percent. Without your employer kicking in, that can be expensive. But you may want to hang onto this insurance until you find other coverage.

You generally have up to 60 days after losing your employer coverage to elect to be covered under COBRA, and coverage is then retroactive. But don't wait that long to either sign up or find other coverage. Remember, if you go 63 days without coverage, you lose important rights under HIPAA. Get information about COBRA as soon as you leave your job so you can make an informed decision.

If needed, you can elect to keep coverage only for your spouse and other dependents who were covered under your employer-sponsored plan. Let's say, for example, your husband has a health problem but you and your child are healthy. The two of you may look for a cheaper individual plan while electing to continue COBRA coverage for your husband who would have a hard time finding health insurance. Get detailed information about COBRA coverage at insure.com.

- *Try the Blues.* Blue Cross/Blue Shield members are large insurance companies, and may offer programs for consumers who can't get insurance elsewhere. Visit their main web site www.bluecares.com for information on a Blue Cross/Blue Shield program in your area.

- *Insure for the worst.* Major medical or "catastrophic" insurance features high deductibles and covers expenses like a stay in the hospital, surgery, intensive care, diagnostic X-ray, and lab tests. If you can't afford the kind of coverage you'd like, it may make sense to consider insuring for the worst—a serious illness or accident. Major medical policies often offer high deductibles of $500 to $2,000 or more. That means the plan pays no benefits until you've reached the deductible amount. Still, it could be a lifesaver; helping your family get the medical care it needs if the worst should happen.

- *Ask your state for help.* Some 35 states fund "risk pools," or high-risk health insurance plans. These plans are generally available for consumers who cannot obtain

29

health insurance because of pre-existing medical conditions. To see whether a risk pool is available in your state, contact your state insurance department.

- *Join the club.* Check with trade or professional associations, alumni associations, or local Chambers of Commerce, all of which may offer health insurance programs for their members. But just because an association endorses a program, doesn't mean it's good. Some large associations have been duped by fraudulent health care programs. Make sure you check out any group plan just as you would any you're considering.

- *Check out Medicaid.* If your income is low, or you've been unemployed for a period of time, you may be eligible for Medicaid. Medicaid is a program under the Social Security Act that provides medical assistance for certain individuals and families with low incomes and resources. Medicaid is the largest program providing medical and health-related services to America's poorest people.

While there are national guidelines that the Federal Government provides, each individual state establishes its own eligibility standards; determines the type, amount, duration, and scope of services; sets the rate of payment for services; and administers its own program. Thus, the Medicaid program varies considerably from state to state, as well as within each state over time.

- *Get Uncle Sam's help.* As of 2003, self-employed consumers can often deduct 100 percent of their insurance premiums. If you're operating a small business, either on the side or full-time, you may want to talk with your accountant to find out whether you can deduct your premiums.

- *Also keep track of your out-of-pocket expenses.* Mileage to doctor's offices, even meals (if you travel for certain types of medical care) may be deductible. If your medical expenses are high in one year, you may be able to deduct those that exceed 7.5 percent of your gross income. Ask a tax specialist for more details.

- *Consider an MSA or an HSA.* A Medical Savings Account (MSA) can give you the benefit of saving for health care expenses along with valuable tax deductions. These policies are usually available to both self-employed individuals as well as groups of one.

- Health Savings Accounts (HSA) create an actual savings account that belongs to the worker, can travel from job to job, and be passed on to heirs. To a large extent, they allow people to choose between health care and other uses of money. Funds can be withdrawn and spent for non-health purposes after age 65, after paying normal income taxes. Prior to age 65, a 10 percent penalty applies.

- In contrast, the MSAs combine a high-deductible plan with a savings account. For example, you may have a policy with a deductible of $2,000 and you may contribute $100 a month to the plan to build up your savings account throughout the year. Your contributions to this savings account are tax deductible, and your earnings in the account are tax deferred. If you use the money in the savings account to pay for qualified medical expenses, those withdrawals are tax-free. If you don't use the money, it accumulates in an account where it can be saved for retirement.

- Advantages of HSAs are:

  —HSAs are portable.

  —HSAs have lower deductible requirements and higher out-of-pocket limits than MSAs, making the accounts more flexible and accessible than MSAs.

  —HSAs, unlike MSAs, may be offered as part of an employer's "cafeteria" plan.

  — HSAs tax-deductible contribution limits are greater than those for MSAs.

  —An employer and employee are both permitted to contribute to an HSA in the same year (unlike MSAs where either the employer or employee may contribute in the same year, but not both).

  —"Catch-up" contributions are allowed for HSAs for people between the ages of 55 and 65 (starting at $500 per year in 2004).

- Shop for these plans just as you would another type of health plan—by contacting local insurance agents or searching online. You'll find helpful details about MSAs and HSAs from AARP.

Lower the Cost of Your Prescription Drugs

- Buy generic drugs when possible.

- Compare how much you are paying for your drugs now with how much those same drugs would cost if you purchased them at another pharmacy in your area or online.

- If you are over 55 and a member of American Association of Retired Persons (AARP), you may be able to reduce the costs of your prescription drugs by purchasing them through the association's mail order pharmacy. You can contact AARP by calling toll-free (888) 687-2277 or by writing to AARP at 601 E Street, NW, Washington, DC 20049. You may also be able to obtain the information you need by going to AARP's web site at www.aarp.org.

Reduce Your Banking and Credit Costs

- Save on fees by choosing a checking account with a minimum balance requirement that you can and do meet.

- Find out if you qualify for free checks from your bank.

- Purchase your checks through a check printing company rather than through your bank or choose to bank online.

- Reduce the number of checks you write by taking advantage of automatic debit options, paying bills online, and by using debit cards.

 Warning

If you use a debit card to pay for purchases rather than using cash or checks, be sure to record the amount of each debit. Otherwise, you risk overdrawing your checking account and incurring bounced check fees. You might also have your banking privileges terminated.

- If your employer will direct deposit your paychecks, find out if your bank will eliminate or lower the fees on your checking account. Some will.

Other Money Saving Ideas

- When you are going to make a major purchase, try to buy on sale and always shop for the best deal. Do your homework.

- If you are purchasing airline tickets, buying them online may get you a discount.

- Take advantage of product rebates.

- Don't pay others to provide you with services that you can handle yourself—yard maintenance, window washing, house cleaning, washing and waxing your car, and so on. When possible, assign some of these tasks to your children, maybe in exchange for an allowance or additional privileges.

- Join a less expensive health club when your current health club contract is up.

- Give up manicures, pedicures, massages, and other personal services. Once your finances improve, you may be able to enjoy them again or indulge in such luxuries on a once-in-a-while basis.

- Get rid of your vices. For example, if you are a smoker or drink too much, stop. You will save money and benefit your health at the same time.

 Warning

A pack-a-day smoker spends close to $2,000 annually to maintain the habit. This figure does not take into account the costs associated with health problems and care associated with smoking.

- Download a copy of the Federal Trade Commission (FTC) publication *66 Ways to Save Money* by going to www.ftc.gov/bcp/conline/pubs/general/66ways.htm.

Some Final Words of Advice

Let's be honest, it may not be easy to reduce your spending, and working more may not be your idea of a good time. However, never lose sight of why you are doing these things—to get out of debt, to build up your savings, to take control of your finances, and to reduce the stress in your life. Also, remember that some of the sacrifices you and your family may have to make to achieve these things may not have to be permanent. In other words, once your financial situation turns around, you and/or your spouse or partner may be able to give up your second job(s) or your freelancing and you may be able to spend a little more. However, no matter what shape your finances are in, you should always live on a budget.

Chapter TWO

What to Do about Your Debts

Married life has not turned out to be quite the way Sharon and Jack anticipated it would be when they got married six months ago. They had expected to be able to buy nice things, travel, and have dinner with their friends, just like they did when they were dating. Instead, they are struggling to make ends meet after racking up a lot of credit card debt to help pay for their wedding and honeymoon. Sharon had always dreamed of a fancy wedding and since her parents could not afford to pay for the kind of dress she wanted, not to mention the reception and wedding cake Sharon had her heart set on, Sharon and Jack agreed that they would use their credit cards to pay for those things. They both wanted their wedding day to be perfect. They also decided to pay for their honeymoon on credit because after considering a relatively inexpensive honeymoon at a nearby beach or in Mexico, they read an article about Tahiti and decided that they just had to go there.

Now, with $20,000 in credit card debt coupled with the debts and expenses they each brought to their marriage, Sharon *and Jack have begun to regret what they did, especially since all they have to show for their credit card debt is an album full of beautiful pictures and a wedding dress hanging in plastic at the back of their closet. To make matters worse, they have begun having trouble paying their bills since the new better-paying job that Jack expected to get did not come through and the sales commissions he is earning at his current job have decreased. Now that some debt collectors have begun to call, Sharon and Jack have decided to schedule an appointment with a counselor at a nonprofit credit-counseling agency that Jack's best friend told him about. They hope that the counselor will tell them what to do to get their finances back on track.*

This chapter explains which bills to pay and which ones to let slide if, like Sharon and Jack, your household income is not enough to pay all of your debts and living expenses. It also provides you with strategies for dealing with your debts when you have reduced your spending and increased your income as much as you can and you still can't make ends meet. Chapter 3 offers specific advice for debts that require special attention either because you risk losing the assets that secure those debts if you do not pay them or because not paying them may trigger other serious consequences in your life.

Tip
Some of the debt-paying strategies in this chapter also apply if you are making ends meet but you have a lot of debt and you would like to get out of debt faster.

What to Pay When You Can't Pay Everything

You followed my advice in Chapter 1 and yet, despite your efforts to reduce your spending and increase your income, you still don't have enough money to pay all of your creditors and cover your living expenses, too. Now what? It's time for you to make some difficult choices. You must decide which debts and expenses you will pay and which ones you will let slide for now based on which ones are the most important. Otherwise, you risk using your limited financial resources to pay debts and living expenses that are not essential to your family, losing important assets, and maybe having to file for bankruptcy. In other words, it is time to do some financial damage control.

 Warning If you follow my advice, your credit record may be harmed, but chances are, if you are in credit hell, it is already damaged. Furthermore, once your financial situation has improved, you can rebuild your credit history so that eventually you have a positive credit history once again.

To control the damage, you should divide your living expenses and debts into two categories—high priority and low priority. For guidance regarding how to do this, read the section titled Put These Expenses and Debts at the Top of Your To-Be-Paid List, later in this chapter. Then use your monthly income to pay your high-priority expenses and debts. If you have any money left after you have paid them, use it to pay your highest interest, low-priority debts. But first, read the next section of this chapter, which explains why some debts are more important than others.

Secured versus Unsecured: What's the Difference?

There are two basic types of debts—secured and unsecured—and the consequences of not paying each type of debt are quite different. A secured debt is one that you have collateralized with an asset that you own. In other words, the creditor has a lien on the asset. That means that if you do not pay the debt according to the terms of your agreement with the creditor is legally entitled to take that asset without suing you first, sell it, and apply the sale proceeds minus the creditor's cost of sale to your debt. If the asset sells for less than the balance due on your debt, you must pay the difference, which is referred to as a *deficiency*. Common examples of secured debts include mortgages, home equity loans, furniture loans, and car loans. Because you are at risk of losing an important asset when you do not pay a secured debt, you should treat that debt as a high priority unless you don't care if you lose the collateral that is associated with it.

Unsecured debts are debts that you have not collateralized with an asset. They include credit card debts, medical bills, utility bills, phone bills, your child support obligation, student loans, and so on. Since your unsecured creditors do not have a lien on any of your assets, they are in a relatively weak position if you don't pay them. Therefore, with a few exceptions, you should treat your unsecured debts as low priorities. The exceptions include your obligation to pay child support, your income taxes, and your federal student loans. The next chapter explains in detail how to deal with these particular debts.

When you do not pay an unsecured creditor, the creditor will probably turn your debt over to an in-house

Exhibit 2.1   Dvorkin's Money Rules

1. Don't be afraid of the word "No."
2. The word "No" just allows you the opportunity to continue negotiating.
3. Get everything in writing. Verbal agreements are meaningless. (Everybody is a liar until they put it in writing.)
4. Unless you want to kill the deal, keep the lawyer out of it until the very end.
5. Always be willing to walk away from a "deal." Don't get emotionally attached to it. Emotional attachment clouds judgment.
6. Don't be influenced by others.
7. Go with your gut.
8. When the money is in your pocket, you're the boss.

collections department or to an outside debt collection agency. However, if the creditor decides that your debt is too small to spend money trying to collect, or if you are *judgment-proof* because all of your assets are exempt and because your state does not permit wage garnishment and does not allow creditors to take the funds in your bank account, the creditor will probably just write off your debt.

Warning

If your creditor writes off the debt, your credit report may be damaged. Also, a write-off or charge-off does not eliminate your obligation to pay the debt.

If you do not pay what you owe after a debt collector contacts you, the unsecured creditor may decide to sue you for the money. If the creditor wins and gets a money judgment against you, he will try to collect on that judgment. To collect, he may ask the court's permission to garnish your wages, seize an asset you own, put a lien on one of your assets, or levy your bank account.

Every state has a law that categorizes certain assets as either exempt or nonexempt. With one exception—the IRS—your unsecured creditors cannot take your exempt assets to satisfy your unpaid debts. Although each state has a detailed list of the specific assets it recognizes as exempt, those assets typically include household goods and furnishings, appliances, a car, tools necessary to perform your job, and so on. Some states allow you to exempt assets up to a certain dollar value. For example, you may be able to exempt $10,000 worth of personal property. Also, in most states, you can exempt a certain amount of the value of your homestead—your primary residence. In Texas and Florida, however, at the time this book was written, you can exempt the full value of your homestead, regardless of how much it is worth as long as certain requirements are met.

Debts and Expenses That Belong at the Top of Your *To-Be-Paid* List

You should treat the debts and living expenses on the following list as high priorities when your money is so tight that you cannot afford to pay everything. If you have any money left after you have paid your high-priority debts

41

and expenses, apply it to your unsecured debts starting with the debts that have the highest rate of interest:

- *Your mortgage or rent.* In Chapter 1, I gave you some options for reducing your housing expense when you are renting and when you are a homeowner. In Chapter 3, I explain the foreclosure process and suggest things you can do to a avoid foreclosure when you can't afford to make your mortgage payments.

- *Home equity.* Any home equity loans or home equity lines of credit you may owe money on as well as any other debts that you may have secured with your home, car or with another asset that you don't want to lose.

- *Your car loan, especially if you need it to get to and from work or to perform your job.* In the next chapter, I explain how vehicle repossessions work and what you can do to avoid repossession.

- *Groceries.* You may be eating beans and rice, but your family has to have food. However, when you are buying groceries, be sure to stay within your budget.

- *Utilities.* Not having heat or air conditioning, lights or water in certain circumstances can be hazardous to your family's health.

- *Phone service.* Doing without phone service can be dangerous especially if you have young children, if someone in your family is chronically ill, or if you live in a high crime neighborhood. However, don't pay extra for "bells and whistles" (like caller ID) or call forwarding and make sure that your service plan is appropriate for your needs.

- *Insurance.* Your mortgage lender requires that you have a certain amount of homeowners insurance at a minimum, and if you own a car, your state law mandates that you have at least a minimal amount of liability insurance—insurance for bodily injury and property damage. Without it, you could lose your driver's license and have to pay a large fine. As for health insurance, doing without it could literally force you into bankruptcy if you or someone in your family is hospitalized because of an illness or an accident or has a chronic illness that requires a lot of care and medication. Chapter 1 provides advice for how to lower your health and medical costs.

Warning Most insurance policies have 30-day grace periods. For example, if your payment is due on the tenth of the month and you don't pay it until the ninth of the following month, you won't lose your coverage. A few companies won't terminate your policy as long as you pay your premium within 60 days of its due date. However, be careful about playing the payment game with your insurance. You could end up being a loser if your insurance is inadvertently cancelled for nonpayment.

Tip On an annual basis, you should review all of your insurance coverage to make certain that you are not over- or underinsured.

- *Prescription drugs and medical treatments* that you or someone else in your family needs to stay healthy.

- *Court-ordered child support.* There are two reasons why you should make this financial obligation a high priority. First, you have a moral obligation to help support your children. Second, if you don't pay your child support, your wages may be garnished, you could lose your professional license, or one or more of your assets could be seized. Also, liens could be placed on some of your assets, which means that if you wanted to sell any of them, you would not be able to complete the sale until you paid your past due child support. You could even be put in jail for not paying your child support. Exactly what may happen depends on your state. Chapter 3 provides a more complete discussion of this issue.

- *Federal income taxes.* If you don't pay your taxes, Uncle Sam may not contact you right away to demand payment but it will only be a matter of time before you hear from the Internal Revenue Service (IRS). Meanwhile, interest and penalties will be accruing daily on your tax debt, dramatically increasing the total amount of money you owe. Worst case scenario, if you ignore the agency's notices demanding that you pay your past due taxes, the IRS may decide to garnish your wages, put a lien on your home or on another asset you own, seize the funds in your bank account, and so on. A better way to deal with your taxes when you can't afford to pay them is to set up an installment payment plan with the IRS or contact them about an Offer in Compromise. You will learn about both of these options in Chapter 3.

- *Property taxes.* If you are a homeowner, you may be able to get an extension to pay your property taxes if you can't pay them by their due date. You may also be able to get your taxes deferred or exempted if you can prove that paying them will cause your family serious economic hardship. Ultimately, however, if you can't pay your taxes, the taxing authority will put a lien on your home and it may eventually take your home and sell it to pay off your tax debt.

- *Federal student loan.* If you ignore your obligation to repay your student loan(s), the IRS can take any tax refunds you may be entitled to and/or garnish your wages and apply that money to your loan balance. Also, you will not be eligible for future federal student loans or grants if you default on the loan(s). In Chapter 3, I provide you with advice about what to do when you can't pay your student loan(s).

Warning Don't pay a past-due debt just because a debt collector pressures to you pay it. The debt may be a low priority debt and if you pay it you may not have the money you need to pay your high priority debts and living expenses. I explain your federal debt collection rights and tell you how to deal with debt collectors later in Chapter 6.

Treat These Debts as Low Priorities

You should treat the debts on the following list as low priorities. In other words, pay them only after you have paid your high-priority debts and living expenses, starting with the debts that have the highest rates of interest:

- *Credit card debts.* If you don't pay at least the minimum due on your credit cards each month, you will lose your right to continue using them eventually. If you need a card for business purposes or to help pay for something that is absolutely essential, then pay the minimum due on one of your credit cards; usually that card should be the one with the lowest rate of interest.

- *Retail store charges and charges on your gasoline charge card.*

- *Bills from your doctor, hospital, attorney, or other professionals (with some exceptions).* For example, if you or someone else in your family is receiving essential medical services from a doctor or other health care provider, then you should treat the provider's bills as high priorities. You should also make your attorney's bills high priorities if you are involved in an on-going lawsuit and you want the attorney to continue representing you. However, both your medical provider and your attorney will probably let you pay your debts to them over time if you explain your situation and work out a payment schedule.

- *Debts you owed to a family member or friend.* Hopefully, your relative or friend will be understanding about the fact that you can't afford to pay what you owe right now. However, it is possible that not paying him or her for a while will damage your relationship. I discuss the drawbacks of borrowing from someone you know later in this chapter and provide you with advice about things you can do to help preserve your relationship with one another under the circumstances.

Warning If you know that not paying the friend or family member you owe money to will create a financial hardship for that person, try to pay at least some of what you owe each month. It is the ethical thing to do.

- *Subscriptions to magazines and newspapers.* Not paying for a magazine or newspaper subscription means that you won't continue receiving the publication.
- *Other unsecured debts as well as all nonessential living expenses.*

Get-Out-of-Debt Strategies

Once you have categorized your debts and living expenses as either high or low priority and have begun making payments on the ones that are high priority at the expense of those that are not, it is time to decide how you will deal with all of your debts over the long term. In the rest of this chapter, I review various strategies you may want to pursue to lower the total amount you must pay on your debts each month to amounts you can afford. Chapter 3 provides specific advice related to some of your high-priority debts, including your mortgage and car loans. The three main get-out-of-debt strategies reviewed in this chapter are:

1. Negotiate lower payments with your creditors.

2. Consolidate your debts.

3. File for bankruptcy.

 Warning When you are drowning in debt, it may be tempting to put your head in the sand like an ostrich and hope that your finances will improve on their own, just like magic. However, unless you are judgment proof and you are willing to ruin your credit history so badly that it will be virtually impossible to get credit in the near future, it is foolhardy not to face your financial problems head on and come up with a plan for paying your debts. If you don't, over time you will have fewer and fewer options for addressing your financial situation and eventually, filing for bankruptcy may be the only one you have left. I discuss this option later in this chapter.

Negotiate Lower Payments with Your Creditors

One of the very first strategies you should consider when you are having trouble paying what you owe is to contact your creditors to determine if they are willing to renegotiate the terms of your debt so that you can afford to continue paying on them. If you believe that your financial situation will turn around soon, they may agree to let you pay less on your debts temporarily or they may let you make interest-only payments for a while. Alternatively, they may agree to permanently reduce your monthly debt payments either by lowering your interest rate or by extending the amount of time you have to repay what you owe or they may completely abate the interest charges. Follow the tips in Exhibit 2.1 for successful negotiating.

If you don't feel confident doing your own negotiating, get help from a nonprofit debt-counseling organization, such as Consolidated Credit Counseling Services Inc. (Consolidated). The agency will do the negotiating for you. Contact Consolidated at 800-SAVE-ME-2 (800-728-3632) or visit its web site at www.consolidatedcredit.org. Later in this chapter, I tell you how to find a good debt counseling organization.

Before you contact your creditors to renegotiate your debts, complete the Debt Summary Sheet in Exhibit 2.2. Having all of the relevant information about each of your debts recorded in one place will make your negotiations easier and will help you make sure that you have not overlooked a debt. You should also review your budget before you begin your negotiations so that you know exactly how much you can afford to pay your creditors monthly. Focus first on your high-priority debts and then on your low-priority debts with the highest rates of interest. In other words, attempt to renegotiate your mortgage and car loans and any other high-priority debts you may have first.

Exhibit 2.2   Debt Summary Sheet

Creditor _____

Amount Owed _____

Monthly Payment _____

Interest Rate _____

Secured _____

Unsecured _____

Collateral _____

Creditor _____

Amount Owed _____

Monthly Payment _____

Interest Rate _____

Secured _____

Unsecured _____

Collateral _____

Creditor _____

Amount Owed _____

Monthly Payment _____

Interest Rate _____

Secured _____

Unsecured _____

Collateral _____

When you know how much money you will have left each month to put toward your low priority debts, you can begin renegotiating them starting with the debts that have the highest interest rates.

Make several photocopies of Exhibit 2.2 to revise your information as it changes.

Negotiating with your secured creditors such as your mortgage and auto lenders can be difficult sometimes because they have liens on the assets you want to keep. The existence of those liens can give them the upper hand in the negotiations since they can always take those assets back—foreclose on your home, repossess your car, and so on.

Depending on the creditor you want to negotiate with, you should schedule a face-to-face meeting or contact the creditor by phone. The person you talk with will be your loan officer, the credit manager, or someone else with the authority to renegotiate the terms of your credit. Let whomever you speak with know that you have been having financial troubles and are having difficulty keeping up with your debt payments. Also, let whomever you speak with know what you have done to improve your financial situation—you are living on a budget, you've stopped using credit, you've sold your second car, you have gotten a second job, and so on. Explain that you want to repay your debt but to do so you must lower the amount that you are paying on it each month. (Be clear about whether you want a temporary or permanent change.) Let the creditor know exactly how much you can afford to pay. Also be sure to get the name and title of the person(s) you speak with.

Tip

It is a good strategy to come up with two different but affordable new monthly payment amounts for the debts you want to renegotiate—a lower and a higher amount. That way, if the creditor you are negotiating with rejects the lower amount you can offer the higher amount, which will make you appear to the creditor as a reasonable person who is willing to give and take a little.

When you speak with your creditors, be polite and try to stay calm. If the person you speak with pushes you to pay more than you can afford, don't give in to the pressure. Calmly and politely say, "That is more than I can afford right now." If your negotiations with a particular creditor go nowhere, don't give up. Ask to speak with the person's supervisor. He or she may have more authority to negotiate. Remember, persistence pays off.

Warning

When you are renegotiating your debts, don't agree to pay more than you can afford. If you do and then you can't make your payments, your creditors may not be willing to negotiate with you again.

Once you reach an agreement with a creditor, write down its terms as well as the name address and telephone number of the person you cut the deal with. Then put those terms in a letter and send it certified mail, return receipt requested directly to the person you negotiated with. Be sure to make a copy of the letter for your files. Also, revise your household budget to reflect your new payment amount and take that amount into account before you contact another creditor to renegotiate your debt.

Consolidate Your Debts

Consolidating your debt involves borrowing money to pay off all or some of what you owe. In other words, you trade multiple debts for a single larger debt. To consolidate, you can transfer the balances on your credit cards to a lower interest card, get a personal loan, or borrow against the equity in your home. You can also borrow against your insurance policy or against the funds in your 401(k) plan and then use the loan proceeds to pay off your debt.

Consolidating makes sense if:

- You can pay off the new debt in three to five years. The sooner, the better.

- The interest rate on the new debt will be lower than the interest rates on the debts you pay off.

- You will pay less each month on your debts. However, watch out for debt consolidation loans that offer very low monthly payments; they usually come with a high rate of interest. Therefore, if you get one of these loans, by the time you have paid if off, you may end up having paid far more on the loan than if you had simply continued paying on the debts yourself.

- You are not swapping fixed rate debt for variable rate debt. A fixed rate is an interest rate that won't change. A variable rate on the other hand can change. For example, it may change if the interest rate is tied to the ups and downs of another rate such as the prime rate, or if you are late by even a day with one of your payments. Therefore, although the rate of interest you may pay initially on credit with a variable rate may be very low, it may increase and, if it increases enough, you may find yourself paying more to pay off the new debt than you would have paid if you had not consolidated.

- The Credit Card Accountability, Responsibility and Disclosure Act (Credit CARD Act) has encouraged card issuers to move toward variable-rate offers. Under this act the issuers must give 45 days' notice before raising any fixed rates many are changing fixed rates to variable rates. As we move forward you can expect this kind of variable rate to become much more standard practice. If that happens, according to the Center for Responsible Lending, the cost to consumers could more than triple.

- People also need to be aware of "pick-a-rate" pricing on variable-rate cards that are tied to an index. Rather than linking to, say, the prime rate and altering what you pay whenever the prime rises or falls, some lenders tie a variable-rate card to "the highest prime rate within a 90-day period." Thus, when rates go down, your variable rate lags behind the move, but when rates go up, you get tagged right away. A study says this one change in how rates are calculated can cost consumers $720 million annually.

- Similarly, card issuers are putting a floor rate on their variable-rate cards, which typically means the current rate has little or no room to drop now or in the future, but has infinite opportunity to rise. Now more than ever you must watch for any changes in terms.

When you are shopping for a loan to consolidate your debts, watch out for:

- Loans that have a lot of fees associated with them. On the surface, a loan may seem like a great deal. However, if you read the fine print in the loan agreement, you may discover that the loan comes with so many fees that its effective cost is quite high. Therefore, it may not be such a good deal after all.

- Companies that misrepresent the terms of their loans. For example, the loan agreement you are asked to sign is not clear about the fact that you could lose your home if you do not meet the terms of the loan or is vague about what will trigger an increase in your interest rate.

- Loans that you have to secure. If you fall behind on your loan payments or if you can't make the large balloon payment that you may have to pay at the end of the loan, you risk losing your collateral. Therefore, before you sign a secured loan agreement, be absolutely sure that you can afford to make the loan payments and be clear about exactly what asset secures the loan and under what conditions you could lose it.

Transfer your credit card balances: A quick and easy way to consolidate your credit card debts is to transfer your card balances to a lower rate credit card; although good credit card transfer rates are becoming harder to find. If you do receive an attractive balance transfer offer in the mail, or one of your current credit cards may offer you a good deal on a balance transfer. Call the customer service offices for your current credit cards to find out. Another good option is to shop for attractive balance transfer offer at CardWeb.com or at Bankrate.com.

Be careful about consolidating your debts with a credit card that offers a very low introductory rate—maybe as low as 0 percent. Unless you pay off the transferred debt while the introductory rate is in effect, you may end up with an interest rate that is higher than the rates you were paying on the debts you consolidated.

When you are shopping for a balance transfer offer, pay close attention to any fees you may have to pay to transfer your credit card balances. If you are not careful, you may have to pay as much as 4 to 5 percent of the amount you are transferring.

If your home has appreciated since you purchased it, you may want to consolidate your debts by borrowing against the equity in your home. Equity is the difference between your home's current value and the amount that you still owe on it. A home equity loan is a quick and easy source of credit that you will probably have to repay over a 10-year to 15-year period. The loan interest will be tax deductible, assuming that the size of the loan is not greater than the amount of equity you have in your home. There is one big drawback to using a home equity loan to consolidate debt— your home will secure the loan so if you don't keep up with your loan payments, you may be at risk for losing it.

Warning When you convert unsecured debt to secured debt you risk losing everything!

Most home equity loans come with a relatively low interest rate. However, be clear about whether the rate is fixed or variable. If you consider a loan with a low introductory rate, don't sign any loan paperwork until you understand exactly what will trigger a rate increase and how much it will increase. If the loan is a good deal at the introductory rate but not at the higher rate, don't borrow the money unless you are sure that you can pay it back before the higher rate goes into effect.

When you are shopping for a home equity loan, pay close attention to the fees you have to pay and the amount of each fee since they will add to the overall cost of the loan you end up with. Also find out if any of the fees will be refundable should you be turned down for the loan. The fees will probably include an application or loan processing fee, origination or underwriting fee, lender or funding fee, appraisal fee, document preparation and recording fees, among other fees like fees for credit verification. Also, you may have to pay points. A point is prepaid interest. Each point is equal to 1 percent of a loan's value. All of these extra costs are important because they will add to the overall cost of your loan.

 Most lenders are willing to negotiate on fees.

When you are shopping for a home equity loan, be careful about the following scams. Unscrupulous lenders who prey on financially desperate consumers use these scams as a way to end up with the consumers' homes:

- *Balloon payments.* You may be attracted by an equity loan offer because your monthly payments will be very low—maybe just interest on the loan. However, if you read the loan paperwork carefully, you will probably learn that you must make a very large balloon payment at the end of the loan. If you can't come up with the money for that payment, you face foreclosure and the loss of your home, which is exactly what the lender is gambling will happen.

- *Equity stripping.* A lender of a home equity loan encourages you to lie about your income so you can get approved for a large loan that you would not qualify for if you were honest about your household income. What the lender is setting you up for is the loss of your home because as soon as you fall behind on your loan payments, the lender will foreclose and you will lose not only your home, but all of the equity you have in it as well.

A *home equity line of credit* is an alternative to a home equity loan. The main difference between the two is that with a line of credit you can borrow against the equity in your home as necessary up to a certain dollar amount— your credit limit. In other words, you borrow what you need, when you need it. The size of your debt payments will depend on how much of the credit line you use and on the rate of interest you are charged. Since your home will secure your line of credit, not making your credit line payments will put your home in jeopardy.

Refinance your home and take money out: If interest rates have dropped since you got your mortgage, you may want to refinance the loan in order to benefit from the lower rates and so that you can add enough money to the new loan to pay off all or some of your debts. Depending on the amount of the new loan and the interest rate you qualify for, you may be able to go from a 30-year to a 15-year or even a 10-year loan without increasing your monthly mortgage payments. However, refinancing may not be a good idea depending on the total amount of the new loan, its interest rate, and duration, especially considering that you could lose your home if you are not able to repay it.

Warning

Taking out a new mortgage is usually not a good idea if you are close to retirement. Don't take this step without consulting with your financial advisor or with a reputable mortgage lender.

Warning

Watch out for prepayment penalties when you refinance. Your current mortgage loan may penalize you if you pay off the loan early since the lender will earn less interest income from you. If there is a penalty, be sure to factor it into your calculations when you are determining whether refinancing makes financial sense.

Get an unsecured loan: An unsecured loan usually comes with a higher rate of interest than a secured loan because there is no collateral for the creditor to take if you default on it. In other words, from the creditor's perspective, an unsecured loan is riskier than a secured loan and the higher interest rate helps compensate the lender for taking that extra risk. For this same reason, most unsecured loans are relatively small—between $5,000 and $10,000.

If your credit record is badly damaged, you may have a tough time finding a traditional lender that is willing to give you an unsecured loan at a reasonable interest rate. Therefore, you may consider borrowing unsecured money from a finance company, from one of your credit cards, from a family member or friend, from your tax-deferred account, or from your life insurance policy. However, each of these options has serious drawbacks. I will review those drawbacks next.

 You may be able to lower the interest rate on an unsecured bank loan by agreeing to let the lender automatically debit your account for your loan payment each month.

Borrow from a finance company: An unsecured loan from a finance company will come with a very high rate of interest—as high as 25 percent—as well as high fees and expenses, which will increase the overall cost of the loan. Furthermore, some finance companies are not forthcoming about the true cost of their loans. In addition, having a finance company loan on your credit record will further damage it because legitimate creditors do not like to work with creditors who have borrowed money from that kind of business. Therefore, consolidating with an unsecured loan from a finance company does not make sense.

Some finance companies make secured debt consolidation loans at relatively high rates of interest. You will probably have to use your home or car as collateral, which means that if you can't repay the loan, you risk the loss of an important asset. Also, some finance companies mislead naive consumers into thinking that they are getting an unsecured loan when in fact, their home or car secures the loan.

 Warning   If you cannot repay a loan from a finance company, it may use aggressive tactics to scare you into paying your debt.

Get a credit card cash advance: Periodically, you probably receive blank checks from some of your credit card companies inviting you to use them to pay bills, take a vacation, or to put some extra money in your bank account. The money you borrow will be applied to your credit card's credit limit. Although using one of these checks is certainly a convenient way to get rid of debt, it is an expensive alternative. Not only may you have to pay a transaction fee, which will be a percentage of the money that you borrow, but you will also be charged a higher rate of interest on the cash advance than the rate you pay on your credit card purchases. Bottom line, using credit card cash advances is an expensive way to consolidate debt.

Borrow from a relative or friend: Getting a loan from a family member or a friend can be a good way to ruin a great relationship. As the saying goes, "A friend is a friend until he asks you for money." On the surface, this kind of loan may seem like the answer to your prayers since your friend or relative won't ask you to fill out a credit application, won't check out your credit record or credit score, and may not charge you interest either. However, step back a minute and think about how your relationship with one another might be affected if you are late with one of your payments or if you can't afford to repay the loan at all.

Warning

Someone who cares for you very much may be willing to lend you money even if it means that he or she won't have enough for themselves. Do you really want to ask your friend or relative for a loan if giving you the money may jeopardize that person's financial security or your relationship with one another?

If you do ask someone you know for a loan, help protect your relationship by working out all of the terms of the loan and formalizing them in writing, just like you would if you were borrowing from a bank. You should also let your friend or relative put a lien on one of your assets. That way, the lender will become a secured creditor, which means that if you default on the loan, your friend or relative can take the asset you have used as loan collateral. Also, if you end up in bankruptcy, as a secured creditor your friend or relative will be better positioned to get at least some of what he or she is owed. I discuss bankruptcy later in this chapter.

Borrow from your 401(k) account: Most employers allow their employees to borrow money from their 401(k) accounts. (A growing number of 403(b) plans also allow borrowing.) Typically, you can borrow up to half of your account's value but not more than $50,000. Some plans limit the use of the borrowed money—to help purchase a home, for educational reasons, or to take care of medical bills, for example.

 Warning If you quit your job or are fired after you have tapped your 401(k) or 403(b) plan, your employer may require that you repay the money that you borrowed right away. If you don't, you will be taxed on it and you will have to pay the 10 percent penalty.

If you borrow from your 401(k), you must repay the money plus interest within five years and make at least one loan payment each quarter. If you don't, you will have to pay taxes on the borrowed money and a 10 percent penalty, too. Meanwhile, until you return the borrowed money to your 401(k), you will be earning less on the account since for every dollar you borrow you will be giving up tax-free compounding interest. If you are close to retirement age, this is a big drawback.

Warning Including the amount that you borrow from your 401(k) or 403(b) account in your taxable income may increase substantially your effective tax rate. Therefore, the effects of not paying repaying the loan or simply liquidating your retirement savings can be financially devastating.

Tip If you have money in an Individual Retirement Account (IRA), you can borrow from it interest free but you must repay the money within 60 days or you will have penalties and taxes on it.

Get a loan from your life insurance policy: If you have a whole life insurance policy (rather than a term life policy), you can borrow against your policy's cash value. The interest rate on the borrowed money will be low and you won't have to repay it according to a set schedule. In fact, you won't have to repay it at all if you don't want to. However, when you die, any money you still owe on the loan will be deducted from your policy's death benefit, which means that the beneficiary of the policy—your surviving spouse probably—won't receive as much as he or she might be expecting. This could create a financial hardship for your beneficiary after your death.

Rules for Filing for Bankruptcy

The Bankruptcy Abuse Prevention and Consumer Protection Act of 2005 makes it more difficult to file for bankruptcy. The banking industry and the credit card industry lobbied hard for this law because in their eyes too many people were taking advantage of the weak laws that were previously in place. There is some truth in that argument. I have seen people come and go through my business who simply did not respect the credit cards they carried with them and charged at will. When they realized they couldn't pay off their bills, they just applied for Chapter 7 bankruptcy and their debts were liquidated.

I don't want to make a sweeping generalization, because some of you got into financial distress because of other reasons, and I respect that sincerely. But you must confront your monetary issues head-on. That's why I'm teaching you the nuts and bolts of becoming a better financial strategist. The majority of people who use credit make a sincere effort to pay off their bills; and if they can't, for whatever reason, it's tougher to file for bankruptcy now. So the gauntlet has been thrown down; and many of you, if you make enough money, will have to pay at least some of your debt. Let's go over it in detail.

Chapter 7 and Chapter 13 Bankruptcy

First, let's go over the difference between Chapter 7 and Chapter 13 bankruptcy. Chapter 7 bankruptcy and Chapter 13 bankruptcy deal with totally different processes; and in the past most people would opt for Chapter 7, which the banking and credit industries believe is the easy way out.

One caveat: This is just a general overview of Chapter 7 and 13. Once you get beyond this section, I will alert you to the new changes in the bankruptcy laws.

Most people recognize Chapter 7 bankruptcy because it deals with liquidation, which allows the bankruptcy trustee to sell off the debtor's nonexempt property to pay creditors—although many Chapter 7 bankruptcy petitioners don't have any nonexempt assets, so there is no sale of property. With Chapter 7 bankruptcy, you can get a discharge of your unsecured debts, such as credit card debt, medical bills, some personal loans, deficiencies on repossessed vehicles, and payday loans.

At the end of your Chapter 7 bankruptcy, the judge will erase, or discharge, all of your unpaid debts, which means that you won't have to pay them. However, you will have to pay any debts that cannot be discharged or that are associated with any nonexempt assets you are keeping. For instance, child support, spousal support, student loans, criminal penalties, and most taxes generally cannot be discharged.

Conversely, a Chapter 13 bankruptcy is a repayment plan based on the debtor's income and living expenses. This means you'll have to prove to the court that you can make your payments. If you don't provide sufficient evidence that you can make the payments, you may be ruled ineligible for Chapter 13.

A Chapter 13 reorganization bankruptcy helps you hold on to some or all of your nonexempt assets by giving you the opportunity to reduce your debt payments and pay off your past-due debts over a three-to-five-year period. Assuming you make all of your payments on time, you will be protected from your creditors during this time.

When you file for Chapter 13, your bankruptcy attorney will prepare your debt reorganization plan, which will spell out exactly what you intend to do about each of your debts. Bankruptcy law requires that your plan treat certain kinds of debts in a particular way. For example, you must pay the full amount of your priority debts during the term of your reorganization plan—three to five years. *Priority debts*, or secured debts, include unpaid income taxes, unpaid property taxes, past-due child support, and spousal support (alimony). With the exception of your mortgage loan, you have two options for what to do about your secured debts: (1) You can keep the asset that secures a debt by paying your creditor the asset's market value plus interest during the term of your reorganization plan. You and the creditor will have to agree on the asset's value, which sometimes can be a stumbling block to pursuing Chapter 13; but if there is no property, then you won't have to worry. (2) You must pay your unsecured creditors at least as much as they would receive if you filed for Chapter 7 rather than for Chapter 13. Examples of *unsecured debts* include credit card debts, unsecured loans, medical bills, and utility bills.

After your reorganization plan has been filed with the court, you will have to attend a creditors' meeting. At the creditors' meeting, the bankruptcy trustee assigned to your case will ask you questions to make sure that you have been honest about your assets and your debts and to determine if you can afford to pay more than your reorganization plan indicates. Your creditors also can ask you questions about your finances. A confirmation hearing will take place sometime later. At the hearing, the judge will consider any objections your creditors may have to your plan and will decide what to do about them. For example, the judge may require you to make specific changes to your plan as a result of those objections before he or she will approve it.

Once it has been approved, *and after you satisfy the additional elements of the new law*, you must pay your debts according to the plan until you have completed the payments. But you must be up-to-date on such payments as alimony and/or child support. At that point, the judge will discharge, or erase, any of your remaining debts except for any debts that cannot be discharged, and your bankruptcy will be over. You will still have to pay the debts that are not discharged.

One thing before leaving the discussion of Chapter 13: You may encounter some bad luck that prevents you from completing your Chapter 13 repayment plan; for example, you could lose your job or become seriously ill and start to make your payments late or not at all. For such a case the bankruptcy trustee may modify your plan, or the court might let you discharge your debts on the basis of hardship.

Get a Lawyer

Unless you've become an expert in this area of the law, I suggest that you hire a bankruptcy attorney, because there will be a lot of work to do—and it's confusing work. Your attorney will guide you through the complex legal issues, have all the numbers in place so you can take the means test, show you your options, and look out for your best interests. A local bankruptcy lawyer can answer your questions about how, specifically, the new bankruptcy laws can impact your debt, whether it's from credit cards, mortgages, medical bills, payday loans, or other sources.

You don't have to go through this painful process alone. And believe me, it's in your best interest to hire a lawyer, because each state, from New Jersey to California to Florida, has different regulations. You can't possibly understand all the degrees of differences while trying to hold down a job, take care of your family, and just survive the day-to-day trials and tribulations of your life. The attorney can also help you decide what kind of bankruptcy you should file, either Chapter 7 or Chapter 13, and will point out the specific advantages of all the property exemptions to which you are entitled (for example, you may be able to choose between your state's exemptions and the federal exemptions) so that you can preserve as many of your assets as possible.

New Rules for Filing

Means Test

Now that the new laws are in place, it won't be so easy to just choose Chapter 7. Before filing, you will be required to do some work. First, you must figure out your current monthly income and measure that against the median income of a family of your size in your state. If it so happens that your income is less than or equal to that median income in your state, then you will be allowed to file for Chapter 7. But if your income is greater than the median, then you must pass what is now called the *means test*. Yes, I know this sounds a bit scary and intimidating, but the lawmakers decided that there were too many people out there generating enough money to pay off at least some of their debt.

The means test is a method used to figure out whether you have enough supplementary income after subtracting expenses called *allowed expenses*—usually such living expenses as groceries, rent, and utility bills, which are necessary to survive—and required debt payments. If you *do* have enough income left, then you will be offered the Chapter 13 plan. So, you must prove that you can pass the means test by subtracting allowed expenses and debt payments from your monthly income. If you can show that the income left after all the math is done is below a designated amount, then you pass the test, and you can file for Chapter 7. Your bankruptcy attorney can help you through the elements of the means test.

Credit Counseling
Before you can file for Chapter 7 or Chapter 13 bankruptcy, you must complete credit counseling and then a debtor education course. This has become a serious process; and along the way, you will need assistance. And even if your bills are so enormous that you will never be able to pay them all back, you will still be required to take part in the counseling and debtor education course.

Before choosing a credit counseling agency or some other agency designed to assist you with your bankruptcy, you should research its experience and what it offers in terms of making this unfortunate process as smooth as possible. The agencies that administer these courses and briefings must be approved by the U.S. Trustee. If the agency you choose is not qualified in this field of expertise, then you could be at risk of failing to file the certification that these courses have been completed in the acceptable time frame. This one mistake could result in the dismissal of your case, and your debt discharge could be rejected. Your lawyer should be able to assist you in picking an agency; but don't be naïve or uneducated. Do some research. A professional agency should provide you with the following while you are earning your credit counseling certificate:

- A web-based credit counseling briefing followed by a short telephone conversation.

- An easy-to-navigate, interesting credit counseling briefing full of useful information.

- A qualified and accredited counselor to walk you through the briefing.

- The ability to stop the briefing at any time to consult with the credit counseling agency or to just take a break, after which you should be able to start up where you left off.

- Customized feedback based on the information you provide.

- A printable summary of the course.

- Electronic delivery of your certificate.

Many bankruptcy lawyers have associated themselves with a variety of agencies to make it easier for everyone and to ensure a somewhat painless process—which includes getting all the certificates, paperwork, and so on filed on time. I recommend using Start Fresh Today because they make it easier for you to complete your pre-filing credit counseling course and your pre-discharge debtor education course in the comfort of your own home. You can find them at www.startfreshtoday.com or at (800) 435-9138.

Personal Financial Management Course
After you have received your credit counseling certificate and have filed for bankruptcy, you must complete, as I said earlier, a personal financial management (debtor education) course before discharge. This course is intended to assist you in planning out your future so you won't slide back into financial ruin.

Your course should be:

- An interesting, informative course followed by a short telephone conversation.

- An easy-to-use program with clear prompts, whether you're working online or over the telephone.

- Clear and understandable financial planning information.

- Flexible enough to complete all at once or in segments to suit your schedule.

- Capable of e-mail delivery of your certificate.

Think positively and take advantage of this financial education. There's nothing wrong with learning more about the intricacies of money management and planning. You won't be able to name many other techniques available to you that can produce a more productive person, in terms of budgeting and saving, than the courses that are being offered by many reputable agencies. It behooves you to take them seriously and, perhaps, to continue to study and learn about the volatile financial world.

Let me share a couple of real-life stories with you. The first is about a couple who came into this process with, in all honesty, a less-than-positive attitude. The second is the opposite side to that story. Don't worry; I'll be brief.

I was immediately concerned for the financial well-being of the first couple because they didn't seem very interested in the process. They thought of it as just another hurdle placed in their way by the government. They were obviously dejected; but more than that, they were angry at everyone involved: the bankers, the credit card issuers, the credit card counselors, and me. Their story was similar to others I've heard before; they lost control of their spending and couldn't keep up with their bills. I talked to them about budgeting, but they didn't think that would make a difference. I tried to explain to them that they weren't alone. Millions of people, for whatever reason, are confronted by money issues every day. It didn't matter what I said; they were not interested.

I did everything I could to help this couple, but their reaction was always the same—they'd do the bare minimum and simply seethe at the process. Let me be the first to tell you that this doesn't help. The laws are set for now, and the process has been simplified to make it easier for everyone. So why not learn from it?

That's my segue into the next story. The second couple was devastated and a bit angry; but above all, they were determined not to let this happen again. They admitted to living beyond their means; and when the wife lost her job, their finances slowly began to deteriorate. They hired a lawyer, researched their options, and worked with their counselors to obtain the certifications required to get their debt discharged. It didn't work out as well as they would have liked; but after all the details shook out, they were pleased with the outcome. The story didn't end there. They both decided to become more financially savvy. They took advantage of the free materials offered on web sites dealing with building budgets, saving money, and living within their means. The anger and resentment that many people feel during the bankruptcy process didn't prevent this couple from spinning a depressing situation into a positive outlook, which is more conducive to success.

Some Last Thoughts on Bankruptcy

For now the Bankruptcy Abuse Prevention and Consumer Protection Act is the new set of rules, and you'll have to deal with it; but you don't have to be alone. Keep your head up, and remember some very important points:

- Hire an attorney. It will save you time and a month's worth of migraines (and you'll have someone working with you).

- Listen to your counselors, ask questions, do your research, and learn. I would suggest that you adopt the same attitude as the second couple. I understand how frustrating this process can be; I live it almost every day. Anger, disappointment, and fear may fill you up sometimes; but please, leave a little room for some hope. No one can take care of your future financial circumstances better than you can, so become your own expert.

- Stop building debt, and start building your savings. It will take time, sacrifice, and dedication; but you can do it, and I will be right there with you to help.

If You Need Help Figuring Out What to Do about Your Debts

If you do not feel confident assessing your financial situation and negotiating more affordable debt payment plans with your unsecured creditors, a reputable nonprofit credit-counseling agency, like Consolidated Credit Counseling Services, Inc. (Consolidated) can help you. You can contact Consolidated by calling (800) SAVE-ME-2, that is (800) 728-3632 or by going to www.consolidatedcredit.org. When you schedule a meeting with a credit-counseling agency, a trained and certified credit counselor will size up your financial situation to determine the best way to deal with your debts. If the counselor advises you to participate in a debt management program and you agree to do it, the counselor will contact your unsecured creditors to negotiate more affordable debt payments for you. The counselor may also be able to get the interest rates you are paying on your unsecured debts lowered and certain fees waived. Once the credit counseling agency has reached agreements with your creditors, you will send the agency money each month that it will use to pay your creditors according to the agreements that were negotiated with each of them. Although it will take time—maybe as long as five years— to complete your debt management plan, if you stick with it, you will get out of debt eventually, especially if the agency requires as a condition of putting your plan in place that you agree not to use credit and not to apply for new credit until your plan is finished.

 Warning Beware of agencies that immediately advise you to enroll in a debt management plan without taking time to analyze your income and expenses. Also be wary of agencies that require you to pay a large up-front fee, and be sure to read an agency's contract and get all of your questions answered before you sign it.

Many agencies also offer other services besides debt management plans. Those services typically include budgeting assistance and educational seminars and publications to help you become a better money manager so that you can avoid financial problems in the future. It is best to work with a credit-counseling agency that offers these services on a no fee or low-fee basis.

Warning

Just because a credit counseling agency says it's "nonprofit," there's no guarantee that its services are affordable or legitimate. Some disreputable credit counseling organizations chose names to make it appear as though they are nonprofit hoping that you will be more apt to work with and trust them. However, they are more interested in taking your money than helping you with your debts.

Ask the Right Questions When You Are Shopping for a Credit/Debt Counseling Agency

Although most credit counseling agencies are legitimate businesses that truly want to help financially strapped consumers deal with their debts, as in any industry, there are some bad apples. If you work with one of them, your financial situation is apt to get worse, not better. Among other things, a disreputable credit counseling agency may not pay your creditors on time and it may keep a substantial percentage of the money you give to the agency to pay your debts. Therefore, to get the services you need for a reasonable price, it pays to shop for a good agency and to ask the right questions. Here are the key questions to ask debt-counseling agencies when you are deciding which one to work with:

- Are you licensed to offer your services in my state? You can call your state attorney general's office of consumer protection to find out if your state licenses credit-counseling agencies. The office can also confirm whether or not the agency you are considering is licensed.

- Are you a member of the Better Business Bureau and what is the phone number for the office that you are a member of?

- Do you offer budget counseling as well as savings and debt management classes? Avoid organizations that only offer debt management plans and that seem overly eager to put you in one before they have analyzed your finances and discussed other ways for you to get out of debt.

- Do you offer free educational materials? Steer clear of agencies that charge a lot for this information or don't have any to offer you at little or no cost.

- Are your credit counselors trained and certified? They should be knowledgeable about money management, debt management, and budgeting.

- How do you charge for your services? Are there set-up and/or monthly fees? Don't work with a credit-counseling agency unless you know up-front how much its services will cost.

- How do you fund your services? Reputable credit counseling agencies receive funding from large creditors like credit card companies, department stores, and banks.

- How does your debt management program work?

- How will the amount of my payments to my creditors be calculated and what will happen if I can't afford those amounts?

- How will you make sure that all my creditors get paid by the applicable due dates?

Warning

Don't sign up for a debt management program you cannot afford.

- How often will I get status reports on my accounts? Can I get access to them online or by phone? You should receive regular detailed statements about your accounts.

- Can you get my creditors to lower or eliminate the interest and finance charges I have to pay? What about late fees? If the agency you are speaking with says it can, contact your creditors to verify that information.

- What debts won't be included in my debt management program? You will have to deal those debts on your own.

- Will I have to make any payments to my creditors before they will accept the payment plan I propose? Some of your creditors may require that you make a payment to your counselor before they will agree to let you pay your debts through a debt management program. If the counselor says you will have to, call those creditors to confirm that that is the case before you give the counselor any money.

- How will enrolling in a debt management program affect my credit? Don't work with any debt counseling agency that tells you it can remove negative, accurate information from your credit record. According to the federal Fair Credit Reporting Act, only time can make that information go away. Most negative but accurate information can be reported for seven years.

- Can you get my creditors to "re-age" my accounts—that is, to make my accounts current? If you can, how many payments will I have to make before my creditors will do that?

- What assurance do I have that my personal and financial information will be kept confidential and secure?

Steer clear of credit counseling agencies that:

- Charge you high up-front or monthly fees to be in a debt management program.

- Won't send you information about their services unless you tell them your credit card account numbers and balances or share other personal and financial information.

- Try to put you in debt management plan without analyzing your financial situation.

- Don't offer to teach you how to budget or help you develop other money management skills.

- Demand that you make payments on your debt management plan before it has completed its negotiations with your creditors.

Resources for Finding a Good Credit Counseling Agency

There are a variety of ways to find a reputable credit-counseling agency in your area. You can get a referral from your financial institution, your local consumer protection agency, a friend, or a family member. You can also contact the Association of Independent Consumer Credit Counseling Agencies at www.aiccca.org or at (866) 703-TRUSTAICCCA, that is (866) 703-8787. However, the easiest way to locate a reputable agency to work with is to get in touch with Consolidated Credit Counseling Services, Inc., at (800) SAVE-ME-2, that is (800) 728-3632 or at www.consolidatedcredit.org.

 Tip Many universities, military bases, credit unions, and branches of the U.S. Cooperative Extension Service offer nonprofit credit/debt counseling programs.

Before you do business with any credit counseling agency, contact the consumer protection office of your state attorney general's office and your area's Better Business Bureau to find out if either office has any claims against the agency, especially claims that are unresolved.

Once you have found a credit-counseling agency you want to work with, get in writing all of the services it will provide to you and any associated costs. Don't rely on a verbal agreement. Always read the contract in full and get all of your questions answered before you sign it.

Chapter THREE

Debts That Deserve Special Attention

Nine months ago, Joanne lost her job when the company she had been working for went bankrupt. Joanne had been a manager with the company and had been earning a substantial salary. She had worked there for nearly six years. Despite her job skills and experience, Joanne has been unable to find a new job that will pay her anything close to what she had been earning. She has worked part time at a couple temporary jobs to bring in some extra income and she has collected unemployment but she is falling farther and farther behind on her debts. She is particularly worried about her mortgage. Joanne purchased her home two years ago. At the time, she knew that she would have to pay close attention to her spending in order to be able to pay her mortgage each month, but Joanne felt confident that over time her salary would increase and as a result, making her mortgage payments would get easier and easier. That turned out to be true; but now, after being out of work for so long, she is having trouble making her mortgage payments, especially since she used up the last of her savings. In fact, her mortgage lender has sent her a couple notices demanding that she get caught up on her past due payments. Joanne is afraid that she will lose her home so she decides to call her accountant to ask him what to do. Her accountant suggests that Joanna contact her mortgage lender to see if it will renegotiate the terms of the loan so that Joanna can hold on to her home. The accountant also suggests that she think about selling her home now that the real estate market has picked up, paying off her mortgage and purchasing a less expensive place to live once she finds a new job.

I f you are having trouble keeping up with your mortgage payments like Joanne is, it is critical that you take decisive steps to deal with the problem or you will face the loss of your home. This chapter describes your options if you are in a situation similar to Joanne's. It also discusses what to do about other debts that merit special attention given the potential consequences of not paying them. Those other debts include other secured loans like your car loan, as well as your federal income taxes, your child support obligation, and any federal student loans you may be paying on.

Most secured lenders do not want to begin repossession or a foreclosure. The lenders prefer to work with consumers to figure out a way for them to hold on to their car or home or another secured asset they are in danger of losing. If lenders take back a secured asset then they will own it, something they typically don't want to do and they will have to spend money to get rid of it.

Dealing with the Mortgage Crisis

A few years ago many people in the United States were persuaded to refinance their mortgages or to take out an adjustable rate mortgage (ARM). On the surface it sounded like a no-brainer—take a 5.25 percent fixed-rate loan and get it reduced to a sexy 1 percent. All they could see was the low payment for which they would be responsible each month. The savings would be dramatic, right? I mean, a mortgage payment that hovered around $1,600 a month falling sometimes to $800 or $900 a month was a dream come true. But something terrible was hiding behind these ARMs—the fine print. Most option ARM borrowers make only the minimum payment each month, thus the monthly savings. They weren't told or advised that if they didn't make the maximum payment on the ARM, the rest of the money would get added to the balance of the mortgage, a circumstance known as *negative amortization*.

 If current interest rates are a lot lower than when you got your mortgage loan, you may be able to reduce your monthly house payments by refinancing the mortgage. However, if your finances are in a shambles and you are behind on your mortgage payments, it's unlikely that you will qualify for a significantly lower rate of interest than the rate you have now, so refinancing may not be an option.

Now, these payment options may not have been fully explained to the borrowers. It has been proven that brokers were paid more to sell option ARMs than other mortgages, and these ARMs would reset after a few years at a much higher percentage rate. When that happened—and it's happening all the time—the borrower was unable to pay the new monthly adjustment. Did the brokers fully warn the borrowers of the higher percentage rates, or did they hide them or let them slide? That's up for debate.

I worked with a family that decided to roll the dice on one of these ARMs. At the time it didn't seem like much of a gamble; it made sense on the surface, but they didn't read the fine print. It just seemed like such a great deal, and the broker didn't offer any advice or caution them in any way; there was no identifiable caveat. After about six months of making minimum payments, they noticed that nearly $1,000 was being tacked on to their balance every month. When they contacted their lender, they were told that they would have to shell out in excess of $8,000 in prepayment penalties to get out of that loan. In a word, they were stuck.

There has been a lot of speculation about whom to blame—the consumers who refinanced without reading the contract or bought a home that was over their financial heads but thought they could afford it with these exotic loans; the lenders for pushing these loans; or the brokers, many of whom, believe it or not, were unregulated.

There is plenty of blame to go around; and I think that as a consumer you should be responsible for your financial situation. With that said, there are tricks of the lending trade; and, yes, they are not fair. The subprime mortgage crisis is another example. This became a bizarre mess. When trying to get a loan in the early days of the subprime debacle, people didn't have to prove their income; they would just state it and demonstrate that they had some cash in the bank. It progressed to a point where the lenders were not interested in the borrowers' assets or what they did for a living. It culminated in lenders giving out loan products to people without the borrowers having to prove or even state the minimum income. The lenders simply required a credit score.

Becoming Upside Down

So, if you were one of those naïve people, you might have looked at this as the American Dream—you could get that house that you had always wanted, even though you couldn't afford it. Everyone was buying, and the prices were rising. If you couldn't afford your mortgage, you took out another one against the rising value of your home. Home equity loans and lines of credit became the norm. But catastrophe was waiting. Maybe you lost your job, or you got sick; or maybe your income just didn't rise at the rate of your debt. Soon you became *upside down*—you owed more than your house was worth because housing prices plummeted. But you still owed that large sum of money that was lent to you.

 It can be hard for many people to admit that they are having financial trouble. However, if you are having problems keeping up with your mortgage, it's important that you swallow your pride and face facts. The sooner you do, the greater your chances of being able to hold on to your home.

You now face a dilemma: Do you sell your house and get what you can and then owe the lender a chunk of change? Do you wait to sell until the housing prices rise again? Or do you allow foreclosure and lose the house? In the end homeowners should make every effort to avoid foreclosure, because it will negatively affect credit scores for up to seven years, making it difficult or more expensive to obtain loans, credit cards, and insurance in the future.

Types of Scams

There is something else you should be wary about when dealing with foreclosure, and that is scam artists. If you are facing foreclosure, you shouldn't trust the people who tell you that they can get you quick cash for your home or fast refinancing without any hassle. Everyone has seen the billboards and signs on the side of the road: "We Buy Homes" and similar declarations. It's not worth the time to call the number or speak to anyone at the number offering help. These people are known as foreclosure "rescuers," and they are not there to rescue anyone but rather to help them drown.

The Phantom help scam. The so-called rescuer will charge people exorbitant fees for making simple phone calls and for filling out forms and other paper-work that they could do on their own. The rescuers don't tell the homeowners this, of course; they make it seem much too difficult for them to do—they want people to rely on them, to trust them. They give people a false sense of security; but nothing is resolved and the homeowners lose their money.

The bailout scam. The rescuer convinces a person to sign over the title to the house with the promise that he or she will be able to stay in the house as a renter, with the option of buying back the house. The problem is that the terms of the buyback are much too difficult for almost anyone to manage financially. In the end the person eventually loses everything, and the scam artist walks away with the majority of the revenue.

The bait-and-switch scam. In this scam the rescuer leads people to believe that they are signing papers that will bring their mortgage current, but they are actually surrendering the ownership of the home. Before they know it, they get evicted and the scam is complete.

The rescuers can even fool mortgage companies. They get people to sign papers, and they sometimes place the ownership of the property into a trust, usually transferring ownership to themselves or to a front person. Mortgage companies are not aware of this, and the helpless people are eventually evicted from the property—and the scam artist could not care less. So please, beware!

Options Other than Foreclosure

Okay, let's shift into a more productive gear and get you the help you need.

Adjusted Repayment Plan
If you feel that your financial troubles are temporary, your lender may permit you to pay off your past-due amounts in a few installments rather than in one lump sum. Maybe you can overcome your financial misfortunes in an efficient manner; if so, ask for an adjusted repayment plan.

Loan Modification Programs
Another option to bring up to your lender is the new loan modification programs. Your lender may adjust the terms of your loan by increasing the amount of time you have to pay back your loan, by lowering the interest rate, or by rolling the deficiency into your loan and reamortizing the new balance. This is to attempt to bring your loan current again.

To be eligible for a program, you must have:

- Experienced a documented hardship or change in financial circumstances.

- Missed three payments (90 days delinquent) or more.

- Owned and occupied the property as a primary residence.

- Not filed for bankruptcy.

You will have to contact the lender that holds your mortgage. This may not be as easy as it sounds since mortgages are bought and sold; but the first place you should look is your most recent statement. Look up the name and make the phone call.

Loan modification programs have been created in response to the housing crisis to assist people with mortgage problems.

- *White House/Treasury Loan Modification Program.* This program was created by the U.S. Department of the Treasury and is comprehensive when dealing with the many types of hardships people in the mortgage crisis are facing. More information can be found at www.FinancialStability.gov.

- *Federal Housing Finance Agency Loan Modification Program.* This loan modification program pertains to mortgages held or serviced by Fannie Mae or Freddie Mac. Loan modification help can be found at www.ConsolidatedCredit.org/housing.

There are many other loan modification programs available. Contact your lender to see what you will need to do to become eligible.

Short Refinancing
Look into a short refinancing of your loan. If your property value has declined severely, the lender may release you from your existing debt and refinance the outstanding balance into a new loan.

Deed-in-Lieu

Investigate a deed-in-lieu. This is a process in which your lender sells your property in order to retrieve a part of or the whole amount borrowed from the sale proceeds. A deed-in-lieu may have a negative affect on your credit, but it still has certain advantages both for you and for your lender. You may be able to get rid of the loan debt, and your lender won't have to spend the time and money on the foreclosure process. If you get released from the loan, you will have to pay the deed tax.

Short Sale

You may also want to explore the idea of a short sale on your home. If your home value has fallen and the loan balance is more than your home's value, your lender could let you sell your home and then take the proceeds. Beware, though: You have to make sure that your lender will forgive the remaining debt.

Horror stories do exist. One family sold their house on a short sale basis. They took the offer because a real estate agent told them it was the best way for them to avoid a foreclosure. Now the bank is coming after them for the difference between the sale proceeds, which were $125,000, and the mortgage balance. Unfortunately, they had not talked at length with their lender regarding the short sale. Take this as a lesson. Do your homework and be diligent. Ask questions and write everything down when speaking with your lender.

 Warning

If your home does not sell for enough to pay the outstanding balance on your mortgage, you will have to pay the deficiency (the difference between what you owe and what you sell it for) unless your lender agrees to forgive it. Attempt to negotiate an up-front agreement with your mortgage lender regarding under what circumstances it will forgive the deficiency.

Housing Counseling

If you plan on obtaining housing counseling, then make certain that the agency you choose is certified by the U.S. Department of Housing and Urban Development (HUD) as a housing counseling agency. One such program is offered by Consolidated Credit Counseling Services, Inc. When dealing with a counselor, this is what you should expect in regard to the housing-related services they offer:

Foreclosure/loss mitigation counseling. A HUD-certified housing counselor will meet with you, establish a budget, and review and determine the best path to either resolve foreclosure or mitigate the effects of foreclosure. The counselor will help you determine the appropriate strategies to get you back on track. Counseling will also offer you assistance in dealing with your lender, provide you information on avoiding scams that may cause you to lose your home, and explain how to avoid predatory lending.

With foreclosure/loss mitigation counseling, a certified housing counselor will assist you in:

- Reviewing your monthly budget, income, and debt, discussing possible methods of budget modification.

- Discussing options available to you for resolving your delinquent payments.

91

- Establishing a workable repayment or other plan that will enable you to bring your mortgage current, allowing you to remain in your home.

- Communicating with your mortgage servicer.

- Submitting a loss mitigation package to your mortgage servicer.

- Creating a written action plan to help you avoid foreclosure and future financial crises.

Reverse equity mortgage counseling home equity conversion mortgages (HECMs): If you are over age 62, a Reverse Equity Mortgage (also known as a home equity conversion mortgage) enables you to convert part of the equity in your home into tax-free income without having to sell the home, give up the title, or take on a new monthly mortgage payment. It can give you access to regular income or to sums of money as needed. Counselors will review your financial situation, determine if you qualify for a reverse home equity mortgage, and help you evaluate other options for increasing income.

With reverse mortgage counseling, a HUD-Certified Housing Counselor will assist you in:

- Reviewing your monthly budget, income, and debt.
- Understanding the advantages and disadvantages of a reverse mortgage.
- Seeing if your goals are achievable with this type of mortgage.

Please note that HECM counseling is *required* before a reverse mortgage can be given. It is one of the most important aspects of this process because it requires an independent third party to make sure you understand the program and review alternative options with a HUD-certified housing counselor before applying for a home equity conversion mortgage.

Prepurchase counseling services: You should meet one-on-one with a counselor to discuss the criteria for buying a home, review mortgage products for first-time home buyers, determine a budget and overall credit history information, understand the steps to buying a home, and learn closing and postclosing information. Counselors can assist clients in preparing an action plan to follow to prepare for homeownership. Documentation usually required for a home buyer preparation appointment will include current pay stubs for the most recent months of employment, two years of tax returns and W-2s, credit information (if applicable), and three months of bank statements. Additional information may be required.

One Last Thought on Mortgages

If you are upside down on your mortgage or are having problems making your monthly payments, try to utilize some of the methods of getting back on track that I have illustrated. Let me make another suggestion: If you feel overwhelmed and not sure of yourself, then get some professional help. It's very easy to get confused and frustrated when dealing with complicated financial situations, and I don't want that to happen to you, because it leads to mistakes and more financial heartaches.

93

As I've stated before, educate yourself; be a smart consumer. Go online and read about mortgages and the new loan modification programs. Talk to your lender and try, even if you are fed up, to be respectful. Losing your temper won't help; bad behavior usually begets bad behavior, and it's better to keep on the good side of your lender while you are struggling through this calamity. Lean on your family and friends for support, and work as a team. There is hope, but you will have to dig in and do some dirty work. You'll also have to sacrifice; but in the end, when things work out for the best, you'll be a better person and a better family because of it.

If you do not feel comfortable negotiating with your mortgage lender, hire a consumer law attorney to help you. The attorney should have specific experience renegotiating mortgages. Having an attorney on your side will level the playing field during the negotiations and will help ensure that your interests are protected in any agreement you reach with your lender.

A talented bankruptcy attorney who is familiar with consumer lending issues can keep a person in his or her home for more than 18 months. However, you will be responsible for the attorney's legal fees, and they may cost you more than finding a new home or a place to rent.

What to Do about Your Car Loan

Depending on the law in your state, your auto lender may be entitled to repossess your car if you miss just a single loan payment. However, in most states, an auto lender won't begin the repossession process until you have missed three consecutive car payments. Even so, the lender does not need the court's permission to repossess your car, nor is he obligated to notify you before starting the repossession process or to give you a chance to pay your past due car payments so you can avoid a repossession. Instead, one day you may walk outside to get into your car and discover that is gone.

Warning

Depending on the wording in your car loan agreement, once you have fallen behind on your car payments, the lender may be entitled to "call the loan." If that happens, you will have to pay the full amount of your loan balance by a certain date, not just the amount that is past due, in order to avoid repossession.

Here are some suggestions for how to avoid repossession:

- Attempt to renegotiate a more affordable payment schedule with your auto lender. The lender may be willing to let you make interest-only or reduced payment for a while, or he may agree to permanently extend the term of your loan so that your payments will be smaller. With any of these options, you may end up

95

paying more interest over the life of the loan, which means that in the end you will have paid more to purchase your vehicle. However, the extra cost may be worth it to you if it means you can keep your car. Also, if you make interest-only or reduced payments for a period of time, your auto lender may require that you make up the difference between what you would have paid on your vehicle during that time if you had been making your regular loan payments and what you do pay with a single lump-sum payment (also referred to as a balloon payment) at the end of the loan. If you cannot afford to make this payment when it comes due, you will face the loss of your vehicle once again.

Warning

When you are negotiating with your car lender, don't agree to anything you cannot afford or don't have any intention of complying with because if you don't live up to the terms of the new agreement, you will end up right back where you started—in jeopardy of having your car repossessed—or worse.

- Sell your car and apply the sale proceeds to the balance on your car loan. If it sells for less than the balance due, you will have to pay the difference unless the lender agrees to forgive it. Therefore, before you try to sell your car, find out if your lender will do so. If the lender agrees to forgive a deficiency under certain circumstances or up to a specific dollar amount, get all the terms and conditions in writing prior to the transaction, if possible.

- Give your car back to the lender. It is called a *voluntary repossession* when you give your car back to your lender because you cannot afford to make your loan payments. After you do, the lender will sell your car at auction, apply the sale proceeds to its cost of sale and then apply whatever money remains to the balance on your car loan. If there is a balance left on the loan, you will be legally obligated to pay the deficiency.

Warning Whether you give your car back to your lender because you cannot keep up with your car payments or the lender takes it back, the loss of your car will have the same damaging affect on your credit history and your credit score. However, for credit reporting purposes, a voluntary repossession may be coded differently than an involuntary repossession. Regardless, either kind of repossession is bad for you.

Before you give your car back, try to get some concessions out of the lender. The worse that can happen is that the lender will say no. It may be open to giving you some concessions because a voluntary repossession will cost the lender less than an involuntary repossession. For example, in addition to asking the lender to forgive any loan deficiency that may remain after your car has been sold, ask it to agree not to report the voluntary repossession to credit bureaus or at the very least, to waive all late fees associated with your delinquency.

Warning Typically, if your lender takes back your car, it will auction it off for less than what you could get for it if you sold it yourself. As a result, you will be left with a deficiency balance—the difference between your loan balance and the auction price—that you will be obligated to pay.

Warning If your lender makes you any verbal promises, don't transfer any assets or exchange any money until an authorized representative associated with the lender puts the promises in writing and signs the agreement.

Getting Square with Uncle Sam

Don't mess with Uncle Sam! If you ignore your taxes, the Internal Revenue Service (IRS) *will* catch up with you eventually and it will collect its money from you one way or another since the IRS has almost unlimited power and time to collect past due taxes. For example, it can garnish your wages, take money out of your bank accounts, put liens on your assets, seize and sell your assets—even your home despite the fact that it may be exempt from the collection actions of your other creditors according to your state's law. Federal income taxes are dischargeable through bankruptcy under certain circumstances. Most of the time, however, the federal government gets its money.

If you cannot afford to pay your federal taxes by April 15, file your return anyway and attach to it an Application for Automatic Extension with the IRS. If you can pay any of the money you owe to the IRS, send it along, too. Paying whatever you can will be seen as a show of good faith by the IRS and will go a long way with the agency.

 The IRS will give you until August 15 to file your tax return and if August 15 comes and you need more time, you can request a second extension until October 15. However, an extension to file is *not* an extension to pay your taxes. Your taxes will still be due on April 15 and not paying them will make you subject to interest and penalties that over time will dramatically increase your total tax debt.

If you cannot pay your taxes, you can ask the IRS to accept installment payments or you can request an Offer in Compromise (OIC). To request an installment payment plan from the IRS, you can:

- File IRS Form 9465;
- Send the IRS a letter requesting such a plan. In your letter, indicate how much you can afford to pay each month and the date you want your monthly payments to be due; or
- Call the IRS at (877) 777-4778.

The IRS will let you know within 30 days whether it has approved your request for an installment plan or if it needs additional information to process the request. For example, if you owe more than $25,000 in taxes, the IRS may require that you complete a Collection Information Statement. If you set up an installment payment plan, the IRS may place a lien on some of your assets in order to guarantee payment of your tax debt. For more information on installment plans, go to the IRS web site at www.irs.gov.

 Warning While your installment plan is in effect, interest and penalties will accrue on your unpaid tax balance. Therefore, you will end up paying substantially more to the IRS than if you had paid your taxes when they were due.

While your installment plan is in effect, it is required that you:

- Make all of your installment payments on time.
- Pay all of the interest and penalties that will accrue on your tax debt.
- Meet all of your future tax obligations to the IRS.

If you don't do all of these things, the IRS is entitled to cancel your installment agreement and to take steps to collect whatever you still owe to it. Again, don't mess with Uncle Sam!

Another option for paying your tax debt is to ask the IRS to agree to an Offer in Compromise settlement if you cannot afford the installment agreement by completing IRS Forms 656 and 433-A. An OIC allows you to settle your debt for less than the full amount that you owe to the IRS. However, the agency will not agree to an OIC unless it is convinced, based on your financial information, that you cannot afford to pay the full amount of your tax debt through an installment plan, either now or later, and not until it has exhausted all other payment options.

You must pay an application fee at the time that you request an OIC. However, if your total monthly income falls at or below the poverty level according to Department of Health and Human Services poverty guidelines, the fee will be waived. To apply for a waiver, file Form 656-A, Income Certification for Offer in Compromise Application Fee, with your completed Form 656.

Warning Your request for an OIC will be denied if you never filed a federal tax return for a previous year(s) or if you are in arrears on the taxes that you owe you for a previous year or years.

Tip Negotiating with the IRS can be intimidating, so if you want an OIC or if the IRS rejects your request to pay your taxes in installments, hire a tax attorney or a CPA with experience handling such negotiations. The negotiation process is very specific so be sure that whomever you hire has extensive experience in this field. You have no guarantee that just because someone is a CPA or has the word "Esquire" at the end of his or her name, that person will know how to negotiate effectively with the IRS.

If you are approved for an OIC, you must file your tax returns on time and pay all taxes due for the next five years, or until the amount you have agreed to pay the IRS has been paid in full, whichever is longer. If you do not comply with these requirements, the IRS will consider you in default of the agreement and your tax liability will be reinstated.

If You Are Behind on Your Child Support

Falling behind on your child support obligation can have bad consequences not only for your child, but for you, too. For example, your state's child support enforcement agency, which is part of your state attorney general's office, will contact you to find out how you intend to get caught up on your payments. Depending on your state, if you can't afford to pay what you owe right away, the agency may garnish your wages, seize and sell your property, put liens on your assets, or cancel your professional license. It may also take any money you may win in a lawsuit or receive in an insurance settlement and apply it to your child support debt and/or take money out of any government payments you may receive such as unemployment payments, Worker's Compensation payments, and Supplemental Security Income (SSI) payments. You may even be declared in contempt of court and put in jail.

 Warning No debt is more important than your child support obligation. A child should not be made to suffer or do without because you can't handle your finances properly, regardless of the circumstances.

If you owe child support, it is highly recommended that you contact the attorney who handled your divorce (assuming you were married) or another divorce attorney when you know that you are going to have problems staying current on your child support obligation. The attorney will file a Request for Modification with the court after which the judge may reduce the amount that you must pay in child support for a limited period of time or may permanently reduce the size of those payments, depending on your financial situation.

 Warning When you fall behind on your child support obligation, your child's other parent may hire a child support collection agency to collect the money you owe. These agencies can usually get faster results than state child support enforcement offices, which tend to be burdened by too many cases and too little staff. Remember, however, these agencies typically work on a commission basis and the money your child's other parent has to pay in commission would be going to your child otherwise so don't let your child support problem get to the point that a child support collection agency gets involved. Take financial responsibility for your offspring.

When You Cannot Pay Your Federal Student Loan

Defaulting on your federal student loan will spell trouble because the full amount of your loan balance will be due immediately and if you cannot pay it, the IRS will help the Department of Education (DOE) collect what you owe. For example, the IRS may take any tax refunds you are entitled to and give them to the DOE so that it can apply that money your loan balance or the IRS may order your employer to begin garnishing your wages. Wage garnishment may happen without any court proceeding happening first.

Warning If you default on your student loan you will be ineligible for federal student loans or grants in the future to help pay for your education. Additionally, if you are a doctor who is receiving federal insurance payments through Medicare or Medicaid, those payments may be garnished and applied to your student loan balance.

The good news is that if you act early enough, you may be able to avoid a default by requesting:

- *A loan deferment.* Assuming you meet certain requirements, you can get your loan payments temporarily postponed. If you have a subsidized loan, the Federal government will pay the interest that accrues during the deferment period, but if it is not subsidized, you will have to pay the interest. However, if you cannot afford to pay the interest as it accrues, you can add the interest to your loan's outstanding balance and pay it off over time.

- *A forbearance.* If you are not eligible for a deferment, you may qualify for a forbearance when you cannot make your loan payments because of a temporary financial set back. During the forbearance period, you will either make smaller than usual payments or no payments at all. As with a deferment you will be obligated to pay the interest that will accrue during the forbearance period, but if you cannot afford to pay it, it can be added to your outstanding loan balance so you can pay the interest in installments.

- *A discharge.* If you get your loan discharged, you will not have to pay its outstanding balance. There are a number of reasons why you may qualify for a loan discharge including: You have become totally and permanently disabled, or you cannot complete the course of study for which you borrowed the money because the school you were attending has closed.

 If you are enrolled in an institution of higher learning, such as a college or a qualified trade school, on a full-time basis, you may be eligible for an automatic deferment until six months after you stop attending that institution. However, be aware that the interest will still be accruing on your loan throughout the deferment period.

Loan consolidation is another option if you are struggling to pay more than one federal student loan. You may qualify for a consolidation loan even if you are in default on your current student loans. For information about loan consolidation, call (800) 557-7392 or go to www.loanconsolidation.ed.gov.

For information on all of your options when you are having trouble making your student loan payments, call DOE's Federal Student Aid Information Center at (800) 433-3243 or visit DOE's Direct Loan Servicing Center web site at www.dlssonline.com/index.asp.

 Individuals who file for personal bankruptcy may not include federal student loans in their bankruptcy because such are treated as exempt debts.

Warning

It is best not to default on a federally guaranteed student loan because the federal government has many powerful tools at its disposal to collect its money from you compared and because you will be responsible not only for paying back the loan but for all collection costs as well if you default on the loan. Furthermore, your loan repayment negotiation options with the federal government will be severely limited if you fall behind on your federally guaranteed student loan. However, state governments and institutions of higher learning that make loans to students have far fewer collection powers than the federal government does.

Chapter FOUR

Using Credit Responsibly

Jake graduated from college a year ago and already he is in financial trouble. While he was a student, Jake was offered a lot of credit cards and he never turned down an offer. Credit cards made his life so easy! He used them to pay for his textbooks, to finance a trip to Mexico during spring break, to buy happy hour drinks for himself and his friends, to buy clothes and gifts, and to take his dates out to nice places.

Whenever Jake reached his credit limit on one credit card, he just used another. He never worried about how much he owed because he was always able to pay the minimum due on each of his cards, so he figured that meant that he was in good financial shape. Furthermore, Jake expected to make a lot of money when he graduated from college, so he was sure that eventually he would be able to pay off all of his account balances very quickly.

After Jake graduated from college, he rented an apartment with his best friend and began looking for a well-paying job. He hunted all summer, but to no avail. There were not a lot of jobs available in his chosen field and whenever he applied for one he was told he did not have enough experience. Meanwhile, Jake continued to use his credit cards to finance the lifestyle that he thought a young, single guy should be living.

At the end of the summer, Jake found a part-time job in his field and began to supplement his income by waiting tables. Meanwhile, however, Jake's financial house of cards was beginning to fall apart. He had reached his limit on all but one of his six credit cards, and he was close to the limit on that one. His monthly income barely covered his basic living expenses, he had nothing in savings, he could no longer pay even the minimum due on his credit cards, and he had begun to get calls from debt collectors. Jake began to regret using his credit cards so freely when he was in college.

As Jake learned, having access to credit is a double-edged sword. It lets you buy now and pay later, which can be a wonderful convenience. It also helps you purchase big-ticket items like a home or a car—things you might never be able to afford if you had to pay cash for them. Credit can also help you finance your child's college education, remodel your home, pay for an unexpected emergency, take a vacation, and so on. But, there are drawbacks to using credit, especially if you are ir-responsible like Jake was and do not have money in savings as a financial safety net. Here are some of those potential drawbacks:

- You will pay more for items that you buy with a credit card instead of with cash unless you pay the full amount of your credit card bill each month. That's because every month until you have paid off your card balance, the credit card company will charge interest on what you owe and because every time you are late with an account payment, you will be charged a fee. Therefore, the longer it takes you to pay off your account balance and the more late fees you incur, the more your credit card purchases will cost you.

- Owing more than you can afford to repay is likely to make you worry constantly and interfere with your sleep. It may also cause you to begin abusing alcohol or drugs and become depressed, and it may drive a wedge between you and your spouse or partner. Certainly, stress caused by too much debt often affects job performance.

- Owing too much to your creditors will damage your credit history and lower your credit score. As a result, credit card companies may increase the rate of interest they are charging you and your life insurance premiums may go up. For more information on credit records and credit scores and how they can impact your life, turn to Chapter 5 in this book.

- You may have difficulty landing a good job if employers review your credit record as a part of their application review process.

- You may have trouble finding a landlord who will rent to you.

- When you have a lot of debt relative to your income, it will be difficult, if not impossible for you to save and invest for your future. Furthermore, if you have an expensive emergency, you may not have any money to pay for it in your savings account, which means that you will probably have to use credit and that will make your financial situation worse.

• You may have to file for bankruptcy.

The goal of this chapter is to help you enjoy the many benefits of credit and avoid the problems. It provides you with basic information about credit cards and bank loans and explains when using credit is appropriate. It introduces to you to the various types of credit, explains how creditors will evaluate your application for credit, and provides advice about how to use credit wisely so you can stay out of financial trouble.

When Using Credit Is Okay

It's almost always best to pay for products and services using cash, a check, or a debit card. But let's face it, sometimes that's impossible. So, here are some examples of when paying with credit makes sense:

• You want to purchase a home, a vehicle, or some other high dollar item that would take you a long time to save up for.

• Your purchase will benefit you long after you have paid off the debt. For example, if you borrow money to weatherize your home, you will reap the benefits of lower utility bills for years to come as long as you continue living in the home.

- You don't have enough money to purchase a product or service that is essential to you, to one of your family members, or to your entire family. Examples of necessities include utilities, groceries, gas for your car if you must use it to get to and from work, life-saving medications, and so on. However, if you regularly lack enough money to pay such necessities, using credit again and again is *not* the solution and will make your situation worse. Instead, get your spending under control by reading the early chapters in this book and following the advice that is given. You may also want to work with a nonprofit debt-counseling organization.

- You prefer the convenience of paying for your day-to-day purchases with a credit card and you make a habit of paying your card balances in full each month.

- You are traveling and a merchant refuses to accept your out-of-town check.

- You need a rental car or want to reserve a hotel room.

- You want to purchase an item online.

- You want to be able to take advantage of the legal protections that the federal Fair Credit Billing Act provides when you pay for goods or services with a credit card. I discuss those protections in Chapter 7.

Credit Comes in Different Flavors

It's important to be aware of the different types of credit so that can be sure that you match the right type of credit to your needs. Otherwise, the purchase that you finance with credit could end up costing you much more than it should. There are four basic types of credit:

1. *Open-end, unsecured revolving credit.* With this kind of credit, you have a fixed credit limit and you are responsible for paying at least the minimum due on your outstanding account balance each month. The minimum will be a percentage of your card's total balance. The interest rates associated with open-end credit can be quite high, especially if you have a poor credit history or you don't shop around for the best deal. Examples of this type of credit include bankcards like MasterCard and Visa and many retail store charge cards.

2. *Open-end secured revolving credit.* The main difference between this kind of credit and the previous type is that you will have to secure your credit card purchases by keeping a certain amount of money in a saving account or by buying a certificate of deposit for a certain amount. Then, if you do not pay your account on time or if you go over your credit limit, the credit card company can tap those funds. Often, people with poor credit histories or no credit history at all must use a secured MasterCard or Visa card until they can qualify for one that is unsecured. Chapter 6 provides more information about how secured cards work and how to select one.

3. *Open-end 30-day credit.* Although this type of credit usually comes with a high credit limit, you must pay

your outstanding account balance in full each month when you use this type of credit. The American Express card is the most common example of open-end, 30-day credit, although the company's Optima card is considered to be open-end revolving credit.

4. *Closed-end credit.* When you are approved for a mortgage, finance the purchase of a car, or obtain a student loan, or some similar purchase, you are using closed-end credit, also referred to as installment credit. Regardless of what you call it, when you use this kind of credit, you borrow a certain amount of money and you are responsible for repaying it over a fixed period of time (the term of the loan) by making a series of regular payments of a certain amount. Installment credit may be secured or unsecured. You will learn about secured and unsecured credit later in this chapter when I discuss collateral.

How Creditors Evaluate You When You Apply for Credit

When you apply for credit, creditors will use three basic criteria to help them determine whether or not you are creditworthy and what terms of credit they are willing to give you. Those criteria are:

1. *Your character.* Creditors will look at your credit history and/or your credit score to determine how you have handled credit in the past. (Chapter 5 discusses credit reports and credit scores.) They will be particularly interested in knowing how much credit you

already have, how often you have been late with your account payments, whether any of your accounts have been sent to collections or written off, and whether you have filed for bankruptcy within the past 10 years. Frequent late payments, defaulting on an account, and filing for bankruptcy will be big strikes against you. Another big strike against you is being delinquent with your court-ordered child support payments.

2. *Your capacity.* When you apply for credit, creditors want to feel certain that you will be able to repay it. Therefore, they will look at how much credit you already have (credit card debt and loans) relative to your income and how close you are to the credit limits on your credit cards. They will also be interested in whether you have applied for a lot of credit recently because if you have, you may be taking on more debt than you can afford. Creditors are typically wary of consumers who have been applying for a lot of new credit.

3. *Collateral.* If you want to borrow a substantial amount of money, the creditor will be interested in knowing what assets you own that you could use as collateral, the value of those assets, and whether they are securing some other debt that you owe. If you don't have any collateral or you don't have enough collateral, you probably will not be approved for the credit that you applied for. A collateralized debt is referred to as a *secured debt.* Your collateral could be cash, a certificate of deposit, your car, your home, or some other asset

of value. When you don't repay a secured debt according to the terms of your agreement with a creditor, the creditor is legally entitled to take your collateral as payment. For example, if you don't pay your mortgage, the lender can take back your home through the foreclosure process, and if you fall behind on your car payments, the business that financed it can repossess your car.

How Much Credit Is Enough Credit?

As we have already made clear, you are asking for trouble if you have a pocket full of credit cards. One or two bankcards, a gasoline card, and maybe a travel and entertainment card like American Express is really all you need. Having more credit cards can harm your finances in a number of ways, including:

- You may be tempted to use all of your cards and, as a result, you may take on more debt than you can afford to repay.

- A lot of open accounts, even if you owe little or nothing on them and have managed them well, will damage your credit record and lower your credit score since as long as they are open you could run up the balances on the accounts.

- Every time you apply for a new credit card, it will show up in your credit history as an inquiry. The more credit-related inquires you have, the more you will damage your credit history and the lower your credit score will go. In fact, currently each inquiry reduces your credit score by four points.

Warning Just a handful of inquiries can mean the difference between getting the credit you need and being denied credit.

You should also avoid having a lot of outstanding loans, especially loans that you have secured with your home. If you can't pay those loans, you risk losing your home.

So when you are using credit, how much debt is okay? As a rule of thumb, most financial advisors say that you should not be spending more than 10 percent of your net household income (after-tax income) servicing your debts, not including your mortgage, car loan, and your home equity loan. Therefore, if your net income (take-home pay) is $2,000 a month, you should not be paying any more than $200 a month on your credit card and other consumer debts. These same financial experts also advise that however much debt you have, you should be able to repay all of it within 12 to 18 months. If you can't, you owe too much. For example, if the combined outstanding balance on your two credit cards is $5,000 with an interest rate of 18 percent and you are presently paying $150 per month on that debt, it will take you more than three years and 11 months to repay it. Therefore, you will need to increase substantially the size of your monthly payments to pay the debt off within 12 to 18 months. For a more in-depth discussion of how to assess the state of your finances and determine whether you owe too much, return to Chapter 1 in this book.

Credit Card Accountability, Responsibility, and Disclosure Act

Now that the President has signed the Credit Card Accountability, Responsibility, and Disclosure (CARD) Act, it may become more difficult to acquire credit from banks and other lenders, simply because they have lost some of the leverage used in the past to crank up ancillary charges, such as raising your interest rates just because they feel like it or because of a default on another bill, which could have been from a simple misunderstanding.

You see, the banks and other lenders won't be able to accumulate as much profit as they did before, because the industry will have to be more transparent. So in the future they will probably be spending an inordinate amount of time and brainpower on discovering new and wildly creative methods, probably devious, to extract more money from their customers. This philosophy doesn't seem to make sense, but the lenders are in it for your money. They simply do not care if you've been an exemplary and responsible cardholder for a decade or more. You would think that a reward for being such an upstanding cardholder would be in order, but that's not the way the lenders operate.

Banks and other lenders will have to explain what they are doing with your account, and they won't be able to exact unreasonable deadlines to pay your bills, thus canceling many of the covert practices that leave consumers wondering why they are getting further and further behind on their monthly payments. This makes lenders angry and has caused much foot stomping and many tantrums in the business.

117

Change in the Credit Industry

Now that the Credit CARD Act has passed, the credit card industry is going to change. You should be prepared for these changes before they happen. As always, be frugal with charging on your card; the less debt you have, the better off you will be—that much has not changed. Credit card companies aren't as focused or as interested in high credit scores, loyal customers, or timely monthly payments as they used to be. They are concerned with risk levels and likelihood of defaults, especially if you are carrying a large balance from month to month. If you pay off your balance each month, they still might be unhappy because they won't be making any money off you in interest charges—so it's a catch-22 situation.

Okay, interest rates are going to rise. You can shop around for a better interest rate because there will always be competition in the credit card industry, but the low-ball interest rates are probably gone for good. Even introductory rates, which were once the teaser to bring in new business, will not be as attractive.

Great balance transfer rates are also going to disappear. Remember when your mailbox was flooded with offers to transfer your balance to a new card with an ideal introductory rate and no fees? Now the rates will be higher, and transfer fees won't be low; and they may not have a cap on them. So do your homework; if you want to transfer your balance, find a card that has a lower interest rate when the initial offer rate is finished. Look beyond the deal.

Annual fees were once a thing of the past; now they are the future. The huge profits garnered from late-payment and over-the-limit fees will not be as easy to accumulate for the credit card industry. So annual fees, and maybe some other new fees, will take their place.

Retailers that offer incentives like "15 percent off or a free product if you sign up and buy today with our card"— such as Home Depot—may go the way of the dinosaurs. Banks simply aren't as trusting as they used to be, and the new laws want the issuers to be more certain of a consumer's capacity to make payments. Many people would look at these deals as an excuse to make large purchases, without thinking about their future ability to pay off the debt. That irresponsibility led to delinquent payments and worse.

Rewards cards may also suffer. There won't be as many big-ticket items, and the rewards themselves won't pack the punch that lured so many consumers to purchase more to gain their rewards.

What the Credit CARD Means to You

The Credit Card Accountability, Responsibility, and Disclosure Act will make it easier for you to deal with the credit card giants. This industry has been running roughshod over its clientele for decades and enjoying the bounty. But there are some aspects that also apply to the cardholder. After all, this bill is about accountability on both ends; for instance, credit card issuers will be required to show you, on periodic statements, how long it will take to pay off your existing balance and the interest you will accrue if you pay only the minimum amount.

Use this valuable disclosure to get a grip on your spending. Be accountable. This is a free educational device showing you, in plain language, what it will take to reduce your credit card balance. If the sirens go off in your head when you look at this information, then you'd better halt your spending and get your finances in order.

Some of the changes because of the CARD Act pertain to:

- *Hidden fees.* It bans arbitrary interest-rate increases and hidden fees, such as charges for paying off a credit card bill over the telephone or online.

- *Full disclosure.* It requires clear disclosure, and in plain language, of the terms of credit card agreements and any changes made to them.

- *Universal default.* It prohibits the practice of universal default, which allowed companies to raise interest rates on a credit card to an outrageous level if the consumer was more than 30 days late on *another* card payment. This was a method credit card companies used to profit off their customers.

- *Late penalties.* Customers must be over 60 days late on payments before their interest rate can be raised on balances. If the rate is raised, it will go back to the lower rate if the customer makes the minimum payment on time for six months in a row.

- *Delays in payment.* It prohibits companies from assessing late fees if the card issuer has delayed crediting the payment. Also, credit card companies won't be able to assess a late fee if a payment is received on a due date that falls on a day when the company is closed, such as a weekend or a holiday.

- *Making payments at local banks.* It specifies that payments made at local branches must be credited the same day.

120

- *Freeze on rate increases.* It prohibits companies from increasing rates on a cardholder in the first year and requires promotional rates to last at least six months. Rate increases must be periodically reviewed.

- *Credit-limit fees or opt-in.* This bans credit card companies from charging fees when users exceed their credit limits, unless the user gives the company permission to go over the limit on the transaction; that is, the user opts to being charged a fee. Regardless, all penalty fees must be reasonable and in line with the overcharge—there will be no more excessive increases for purchases that narrowly went over the credit limit. If the cardholder has not agreed to allow the transaction to go over the limit, then it would be rejected.

- *Early-morning deadlines.* It prohibits issuers from setting an early-morning deadline for credit card payments, because they usually receive their mail in the afternoon. This was another shady practice by the credit card companies to make a buck off their customers.

- *Statements and notifications.* The CARD Act notes that credit card statements must be mailed 21 days before the bill is due. The old requirement was a short 14 days, which sometimes made it impossible to receive the bill, look it over, and then mail the payment on time. Also, consumers must now be given 45 days' notice of any fee, rate, or penalty increases. Under the old rules, credit card companies could raise rates for any reason and with only 15 days' warning.

- *Application of overpayments.* Another method credit card companies used to make more money off their

121

customers was to apply extra payments to balances with the lowest interest rates. The higher-interest-rate balance would not have any of the payment allocated toward it and would accrue interest on the unpaid amount and result in a larger balance. Now payments over the minimum must be applied first to the credit-card balance with the highest rate of interest, helping the consumer to wipe out that burden more quickly.

- *Plain language in plain sight.* Banks and lenders will give consumers clear disclosures of account terms before consumers open an account and clear statements of the activity on their accounts afterward. This means that fees that you have been charged will be highlighted on statements, and these statements will also clearly show fees you have paid in the current month and the year-to-date amounts as well as the reasons for those fees. Use this as an educational tool to help you manage your finances and to correct any mistakes you have been making in order to wipe out these fees.

- *Gift cards.* They will not be allowed to expire for five years, and the credit card companies will not be permitted to charge dormancy fees on the balance left on the card.

- *Fair disclosure.* This mandates that credit card companies must reveal the time and the total interest costs it would take to pay off credit card balances, if the customers paid only the required minimum.

- *Protection for students.* The act contains new protections for college students and adults under the age of 21. Universities will have to disclose their agreements and relationships with credit card issuers with regard to the marketing or distribution of credit cards to students. Many lenders have established relationships with universities in order to get on campus and dupe those students who are naïve to the credit industry.

- *Public posting of credit card contracts.* The run-of-the-mill hard-copy contracts must now be in plain language and available on the Internet in a usable format. This will make it fundamentally easier for regulators and consumer advocates to scrutinize changes in credit card terms and to assess whether the disclosures and protections are sufficient.

The Future Just Arrived

Now that the changes have been made, it's time to prepare for your financial future in regard to credit cards. As always, you should carefully look through your bills and account information to see if any changes have been made, such as credit limits or rate hikes. Being an informed consumer is your best defense; and it should be much easier now, with most surprise devices stripped from lenders, to spot any transgressions on your financial status.

If you are in significant trouble right now, you may want to consider speaking with a credit counseling agency. Banks want their money, and they won't be as brutal on those consumers who are at least making an effort to pay the money that they owe. A credit counseling agency can assist you in setting up reasonable monthly payments to help revitalize your financial health.

The last and most important element of this whole matter drills down to one thing—accountability. As a credit card user, it is up to you to take matters into your own hands. Yes, there are moments when you must use your credit card for an emergency situation or situations, and that could devastate your finances. That is completely understood. But many times credit card debt is due to spending beyond your means. As a consumer you can make the Credit CARD Act work for you by controlling your spending and keeping your monthly balance to a minimum.

You can turn the tables now by paying more attention to your monthly bills and by taking advantage of the periodic disclosures showing you, in plain language, how long it will take to pay off your balance by making the minimum payment (of course, increase that payment if you can). Remember, the Credit CARD Act was established to protect you from the sly tactics of credit card lenders and to provide you with tools to better manage your credit card spending. So as a credit card holder, you've been given an opportunity, and with that opportunity comes the added responsibility to make it work for you.

Think of the Credit CARD Act as an extraordinary event that furnishes you with the chance to enhance your financial position in the world, no matter how small or large it is, and to finally stay one step ahead of an industry that has long prided itself on creating debt rather than savings. Then you'll be the one laughing as your savings go up and your debt goes down.

When You Are in the Market for a Credit Card

There are good credit cards and there are bad ones. Good credit cards have attractive terms of credit so they cost less to use than bad ones. Therefore, when you are in the market for a credit card, your goal should be to find a card with attractive terms. The federal Fair Credit and Charge Card Disclosure Act (FCCCDA) makes this relatively easy to do because it requires credit card companies to provide you with specific information about the terms of their offers allowing you to compare offers. The FCCCDA-required information includes a card's:

- *Annual percentage rate (APR).* This is the amount of interest you will pay annually on your credit card balance. The higher the APR, the more you will pay to use a card, assuming you do not pay off your card balance each month.

- *Periodic rate.* This is the daily rate of interest you will pay on your outstanding card balance. It is calculated by dividing a card's APR by 12 months. For example, if a card has an APR of 18 percent, its periodic rate is 1.5 percent. Although when expressed as a periodic rate, a card's rate of interest may not seem high, if you maintain a balance on the card from month to month, the amount of interest you pay will really add up over time.

- *Grace period.* This is the amount of time you will have to pay your full credit card account balance before interest will start accruing. Some cards have no grace period. That means that even if you pay the card's full balance by the due date, you will still be charged interest.

Warning The interest rate for credit card cash advances is almost always higher than the one that applies to purchases. Also, most card issuers begin charging interest on a cash advance as soon as you receive it.

- *Balance calculation method.* This is the method used by a card issuer to calculate the amount of interest you will pay on your account balance each month. There are six different methods and some of them will cost you more than others. From the least expensive method to the most expensive balance calculation method, they are:
  —Adjusted balance
  —Average daily balance excluding new purchases
  —Previous balance
  —Average daily balance including new purchases
  —Two-cycle average daily balance excluding new purchases
  —Two-cycle average daily balance including new purchases

- *Fees.* The more fees that apply to a card and the higher the fees, the more it will cost you to use it. The fees may include:
  —An annual fee for the right to use a card
  —A late fee
  —A fee for exceeding your credit limit

—A balance transfer fee

—A cash advance fee

To ensure that you get the best deal possible on a credit card, take time to read and compare the terms of various credit offers you receive in the mail or learn about on the Internet. Don't rely on a credit card company's marketing flyer or letter, which are intended to point out a card's good points and gloss over its negatives. However, "the devil is in the details" and you will find those details in the fine print.

Be proactive when you shop for credit. Don't assume that the offers that arrive in your mailbox are the best ones you can qualify for. Instead, go to www.bankrate.com and www.cardtrak.com. Each web site features information about good deals on credit cards. You can also call CardTrak at (800) 344-7714 to order a list of low interest credit cards.

When you shop for a credit card offer, avoid cards that:

- Charge you a fee each time you use them.

- Charge you a fee for not using your card enough.

- Have annual fees that escalate over time.

- Offer an initial interest rate that starts out low and then escalates after a relatively short period of time—six months typically—unless the higher rate is still lower than other cards you can qualify for.

Warning

If you transfer your credit card balances to a new card in order to take advantage of its low introductory interest rate, unless you pay off the transferred balance before the card's interest rate goes up, you may end up spending more to pay off the transferred debt than if you had not done the balance transfers.

- Offer you rewards. Although you may be attracted to the idea of earning frequent flier miles or some other type of benefit by using a reward card, this type of card usually has a higher than average interest rate. Furthermore, unless you run up a large balance on the card, it will probably be years before you have enough points accrued to be able to benefit from the rewards.

Warning

Before you transfer a credit card balance, read and understand all of the terms and conditions of the card you are transferring to before you complete the transaction.

Consider How You Will Use a Credit Card

When you are evaluating credit card offers, take into account how you intend to use the card. That's because whether or not you intend to carry a card balance from month to month or plan on paying your full balance each month will make some terms of credit relatively more important than others. For example, if you plan to pay off your credit card balance each month, you want a card with a no/low annual fee and a long grace period—at least 25 days. However, if you intend to maintain a balance on your credit card, then look for a card with a low APR and a consumer-friendly balance calculation method.

Once You Have a Credit Card, Use It Wisely

Once you are approved for credit, following the practical advice in this section of the chapter will help you manage it wisely. I have already provided some of this advice in other chapters but it is important enough to repeat:

- Pay your credit cards according to the terms of your credit card agreements.

- Consider paying your credit cards online or over the telephone to avoid being late with your payments and incurring late fees. Being late will damage your credit record as well as your credit score. Also, depending on the terms of your credit card agreements, being late with just one account payment could trigger a steep increase in your interest rates.

 Warning

Watch out for credit card agreements that entitle the credit card company to raise your interest rate if your credit history shows that you were late paying some of your bills even if you have been paying your credit card on time. This provision is called a *universal default clause.*

- Don't run up the balances on your credit cards. Ideally, when you make a credit card purchase, you will not charge anything more on the card until you have paid off your account balance. If you do maintain a balance on your credit card, always pay more than the minimum due so that you can pay off the card sooner, not later. The longer you take, the more your credit card will cost you.

 If you can't pay the balance in full on each of your credit cards, focus on paying off your highest interest rate cards first. Once you have paid the balances on those cards in full, put the money you were paying on them toward the card(s) with the next highest interest rates.

- Cancel any retail charge cards you may have and pay off their balances. Nearly all retailers accept MasterCard and Visa so there is no reason to have a retail charge card. On top of that, retail cards tend to have relatively high interest rates.

- Look through the flyers that come with your monthly credit card billing statements. Most of the inserts will probably be marketing solicitations, but some of them may notify you of changes in the terms of your credit—charges that will almost certainly be good for the card issuer but not for you. Other inserts may notify you of your right to opt out of having the credit card company share your personal and financial information with other companies, and tell you how to opt out. Take advantage of these opportunities because the less your information is shared among businesses, the less likely that you will be the victim of identity theft and the fewer unwanted marketing solicitations you will receive in the mail. By the way, credit card issuers are not obligated to give you any more than 15 days notice before they change the terms of your credit.

- Don't take advantage of skip payment offers. You will be charged interest on your outstanding card balance for the month you skip making a payment, so the total outstanding balance on your credit card will increase even if you do not charge anything more on the card.

- Don't go over your credit limit. Exceeding that limit or getting close to it will damage your credit history and lower your credit score.

- Minimize your use of cash advances. Although a cash advance is a quick source of extra cash, it is also an expensive source since the interest rate applied to a cash advance balance will be significantly higher than the one that applies to your purchases. Also, you may be charged a steep one-time fee for each cash advance. These same pitfalls apply to the "convenience checks" you may receive periodically from credit card companies.

- Avoid credit card offers for travel insurance, collision insurance, life insurance, extended warranties, emergency road service, and so on. They are often unnecessary and you can almost always buy them for less from another source.

131

- Don't buy credit card insurance. When you purchase this kind of insurance through a credit card company, your card payments will be made for you if you become disabled and you can't satisfy your financial obligations. The insurance will also pay off your credit card debt if you die. The problem with this kind of insurance is that it tends to be highly priced and generates big profits for card issuers. A better way to protect yourself from the financial impact of unemployment or disability is to build up your savings and maintain zero or low balances on your credit cards. Another alternative is to purchase disability insurance and possibly a term policy.

- Consider whether it's worth the money to register your credit cards with a special service in order to protect yourself from unauthorized charges in the event your cards are lost or stolen, especially if you carry just a few credit cards. The federal Fair Credit Billing Act says that if you notify a card issuer as soon as you realize that your card has been lost or stolen, you won't have to pay any unauthorized charges. The law also says that if you don't realize right away that your card has been lost or stolen and unauthorized charges appear on your card as a result, the most you will have to pay is $50. Certainly, a card registry service is a nice convenience since it will take just one call—to the card registry service—to report that your cards have been lost or stolen rather than having to make separate calls to each of your credit card companies. However, is the convenience really worth the expense, especially if you have few credit cards?

You can create your own no cost credit card registry for free by recording information about each of your cards in a file on your computer, or for safety reasons, put the information in a secure place within the confines of your home. Note the name of each credit card company, each account number, and the toll-free numbers to call should any of the cards become lost or stolen.

Getting a Loan

There are two basic types of loans—unsecured and secured loans. An unsecured loan is one that you do not have to collateralize with an asset. After your loan application is approved, all you have to do is sign on the dotted line. Therefore, to help protect themselves against the financial repercussions of a possible default, most lenders only make unsecured loans for relatively small amounts of money and often charge relatively high rates of interest.

A secured loan works quite differently. The lender will require you to secure it with one of your assets so that the lender can take the asset if you default on the loan. The greater the amount of money you want to borrow, the more likely your loan will be secured. Common examples of secured loans include mortgages, home equity loans, and car loans.

If your credit history is ruined, it may be difficult for you to get new credit. In this case, reputable lenders may only be willing to give you a secured loan, even if you want to borrow just a small amount of money.

No matter what type of loan you apply for, the federal Truth in Lending Act requires lenders to provide you with certain written information before you sign a loan agreement so that you understand the exact terms of the loan. Among other things, the written information must indicate:

- The terms of the loan, including the amount of the loan, the amount of interest you will pay over the life of the loan, and the cost of any loan-related fees associated with the extension of credit.

 Tip If you must purchase credit insurance as a condition of a loan, shop around for the best deal. You do not have to buy the insurance from the lender.

- Whether you must pay a down payment and if so, how much you must pay.
- The loan's annual percentage rate or APR.
- The loan's periodic rate—the rate of interest you will pay each day on the loan's outstanding balance.
- Any conditions that will cause the loan interest rate to increase.
- The total amount of finance charges you will pay over the life of the loan unless you pay it off early.

134

- The total number of payments required to pay off the loan unless you pay it off early.

- The loan payment schedule and when the loan will be paid off according to that schedule.

- The amount of each loan payment.

- The amount of the late fee.

- Whether you must make a balloon payment, a large, lump sum payment, at the end of the loan term.

- Whether you must pay a penalty if you want to pay the loan off early.

Tip

If you are approved for a home equity loan, a home equity line of credit, or for any other kind of credit where you use your home as collateral, after you have signed the loan agreement, the lender must give you until midnight of the third business days (Saturdays included) to change your mind and cancel the loan.

Chapter FIVE

Credit Reporting Agencies, Credit Reports, and Credit Scores

Jack and Nancy left their meeting with the mortgage broker shaking their heads in disbelief. They had been living on a strict budget and working extra jobs for several years with the goal of being able to make a down payment on a home and they had found a modestly priced home in their area that they wanted to buy.

Jack and Nancy were nervous but excited when they walked into the mortgage broker's office, but they were totally unprepared for what they learned after he reviewed their credit histories online. The broker told Jack and Nancy that they would not qualify for a mortgage with attractive terms because there was too much negative information in their credit histories. He printed off copies of those histories for Jack and Nancy so they could see for themselves exactly what stood in their way of home ownership. After reviewing the problem accounts, Jack and Nancy told the mortgage broker that they did not recognize any of the enemies. The problem accounts did not belong to them! The broker responded that their credit identities may have been stolen and that they would not be able to qualify for a good mortgage as long as all of that negative information was in their credit files. He told them to clear up the problems and then come back to see him.

As Jack and Nancy found out, the information in your credit record can have a big impact on your life. In fact, perhaps no other record can have as profound an affect on your life—for good or bad. If the information in your credit record is positive, it will be easier for you to get credit at reasonable terms. However, if the information is negative, you may be denied credit. Also, you may be turned down for a new job or promotion, it may be difficult for you to purchase adequate life insurance, or the cost of your premium may be increased. Negative credit record information can also affect your ability to rent a nice place to live and to qualify for a government permit, professional license, a security clearance, or certain government benefits. However, despite this gloomy scenario, there is some good news when your credit history is full of negatives. The good news is that a bad credit history won't haunt you forever because, by law, most negative information can only remain in your credit record for seven years, which means that over time you can build a new positive credit history for yourself. In this chapter, I offer you a credit record crash course. I explain how to put your credit record in order and how to correct any problems you may find in it. I also highlight your credit record rights under the federal Fair Credit Reporting Act (FCRA) and the laws that have amended it, which include the Consumer Credit Reporting Reform Act (CCRRA), which was passed in 1996, and the Fair and Accurate Credit Transactions Act (FACTA), which Congress passed in 2003. I also discuss the growing importance of credit scores and provide tips for raising yours. Read Chapter 6 to find out how to rebuild your credit.

What Is a Credit Reporting Agency?

A credit reporting agency, also known as a credit bureau, is a business that collects information about consumers' use and management of their credit. It gets its information from a variety of sources including creditors and court records. In turn, it sells its information to creditors, employers, landlords, and government agencies and to anyone else who is legally entitled to it according to the FCRA.

Three corporate giants dominate the credit reporting industry. They are Equifax, Experian, and TransUnion. Between them, these companies collect information on nearly every American consumer. Therefore, if you have credit or have ever used credit in the past, each of these companies probably has information about you.

 Warning The information in the reports being maintained about you by each of the three national credit bureaus is probably not exactly the same although much of it may be identical.

What's in Your Credit Record?

Your credit record (also referred to as a credit file, credit report, or credit history), contains four basic types of information:

1. Identifying information, including your name, address, Social Security number, the name of your spouse, and the name of your current employer.

2. Information about your credit accounts. This section of your credit report provides a detailed history of how you have managed your accounts over time. Among other things, it indicates the date you opened each account, if and when you have ever exceeded your credit limits, your current account balances, your monthly payment amounts, how often you have been late with your account payments, whether any of your accounts have been sent to collections or written off, and so on. This is the heart of your credit record.

3. Public record information including information about any bankruptcies you may have filed over the past 10 years, unpaid tax liens, court judgments against you, and so on.

4. Information about any inquiries regarding your credit record information. The inquiries could be the result of your applying for new or additional credit, or because a creditor or insurance company wants to send you a pre-approved offer. The inquiries could also exist because your current creditors checked out your credit history to determine whether they should change the terms of your accounts, increase your credit limits, or some other action.

Credit reporting agencies get most of their information from their subscribers—the businesses that pay credit bureaus for the right to regularly access the information in their databases. Some subscribers, including bankcard companies like MasterCard and Visa, mortgage lenders, and large retailers, provide credit reporting agencies with regular monthly updates regarding the status of their account holders. Generally however, utilities, hospitals, smaller retailers, auto dealers, and landlords only report information when a consumer's account is past due, has been turned over to collections, or when they have obtained a court judgment against a consumer because the consumer did not live up to the terms of his or her agreement with them. Some gas card companies and credit unions report information about their account holders every month while others do so only when a consumer's credit account becomes past due. Smaller lenders, such as "Buy here/Pay here" car lots, generally do not report to credit bureaus at all since there is no law requiring them to do so.

Warning If there is positive information missing from your credit report, creditors are not required to add what is missing to your report just because you ask them to do so. In other words, you really have little control over what does and does not get reported to credit bureaus.

If you manage your credit responsibly and all of the information in your credit file is accurate, you will have a positive credit history. However, if your credit file contains a lot of negative information, just the opposite will be true.

Tip FACTA says that when a creditor adds new negative information to your credit record it must inform you of that fact in writing no later than 30 days after the information has been added.

Notification can be made via your account billing statement, a default notice, or through some other document provided by the creditor.

Who Can Check Out Your Credit Record Information

The FCRA limits who can have access to your credit record information (or obtain your credit score) and defines under what circumstances businesses and other organizations can do so, for example:

- Creditors can review the information in your credit file in order to help them determine whether or not to give you new or additional credit and what terms to offer you, whether to change your credit limit or to cancel your account. They can also look at your information in order to decide if they should write off a past due debt or turn it over to collections.

- Insurance companies can look at your credit file to help them decide if they want to sell you new or additional insurance and whether to increase your premium.

 Warning There is a high correlation between having a bad driving record and a poor credit history.

- Employers can check out your credit record information in order to determine whether or not to hire you, promote you, demote you, or fire you. However, they must get your permission first.

- Investors and loan servicing companies can look at your consumer credit record information to help them evaluate the risks associated with an existing obligation you have with them.

- State and local child support enforcement agencies can review the information in your credit record to help them decide how much child support you must pay and to help them enforce a court order obligating you to pay child support.

- Businesses or individuals who have your written permission to review your credit history.

- Someone with a court order that entitles them to look at your credit record information.

- The federal government if it thinks that you may be a risk to homeland security.

- The IRS if it has a subpoena to review the information in your credit file.

- Anyone with a legitimate business need to review your credit file in connection with a business transaction that you initiate.

- You have a right to review your credit record information at any time.

How to Find Out What Is in Your Credit Report

The FCRA gives you certain rights when it comes to your credit record. Exhibit 5.1 (beginning on p. 148) summarizes those rights. One of the most important is the right to know what is in your credit record. Since new information is constantly being added to it, you should order a copy of your credit record from each of the three national credit bureaus every six months so you can be sure that all of the information is accurate. You should also review your credit records before you apply for important credit; a new job or promotion; a place to rent; or a government license, security clearance, or government benefit.

 Tip You are entitled to receive your credit report for free once a year. Go to annualcreditreport.com and follow the instructions to get your reports. Do not go to freeannualreport.com, as they charge a fee!

 Warning Computerized credit history scoring systems will lower your credit score and harm your credit record each time your credit file is reviewed for credit granting purposes. Therefore, don't apply for credit you don't really need.

It is important to order a copy of your credit report from all three of the national credit bureaus, not just from one, because each credit bureau is likely to have slightly different information about you in its database. Three reasons for this are:

1. Credit bureaus get most of their information from their subscribers and they do not share all of the same subscribers. Therefore, accounts that appear in the credit report generated by one of the three national credit reporting agencies may not be in the reports produced by the other two.

2. There may be different errors and problems in the credit files each credit reporting agency is maintaining on you.

3. Reviewing each of your credit records regularly helps protect you against the financial impact of being the victim of identity theft, which is a federal crime. Identity theft occurs when someone steals your personal and/or financial information in order to drain your bank account, charge up your credit accounts, open new credit accounts in your name but without your authorization, and so on. Unless you check out the information in your credit files on a regular basis, you may not know that your identity has been stolen until you begin getting calls and letters from creditors or debt collectors asking you to pay debts you do not know about and did not incur. At that point, your credit record will already have been damaged.

Most credit bureaus, including Equifax, Experian, and TransUnion, delete Chapter 13 bankruptcies from consumer credit files after seven years.

Your state may have its own credit reporting law and that law may provide for stiffer penalties for violators than does the FCRA or the two laws that amended it. Therefore, when your rights have been violated, your attorney may want to file a lawsuit in your state's court rather than in federal court. Whether you can sue in your state's court will depend on how your rights were violated.

How to Order Your Credit Reports

If you have already obtained your credit reports and want to order additional copies of the reports, you must contact each credit bureau individually by phone, mail, or online. Here is their contact information:

Equifax
Information Services LLC
P.O. Box 740241
Atlanta, Georgia 30374
(800) 685-1111
www.equifax.com

Experian
They now only offer credit reports online or over the phone.
(888) 397-3742
www.experian.com/yourcredit

TransUnion
2 Baldwin Place
P.O. Box 2000
Chester, Pennsylvania 19022
(800) 888-4213
www.transunion.com

To avoid a delay when ordering your credit report by mail, be sure to include the following information in your request letter:

- Your full name, including your middle name. Be sure to note whether you are a "Jr.," "Sr.," "III," and so forth, if applicable

- Your spouse's name, if you're married

- Your date of birth

- Your Social Security number
- Your current address and former address, if you've lived at your current address for less than five years
- The name of your current employer
- Your daytime and evening phone numbers with area codes

The Cost of Your Credit Report

As you have already learned, FACTA entitles you to a free annual credit report upon request from each of the three national credit reporting agencies and you are also entitled to a free credit report under specific circumstances. However, if you want to order copies of your credit reports when federal law does not provide for a free report, the cost per credit report in most states at the time this book was written is $10.50. Some states may add sales tax to the total cost. Also, some states entitle their residents to reduced cost or free credit reports (in addition to the free annual report). Those states are:

California: $8.00 for each report

Colorado: One free copy a year; $8.00 for each additional copy

Connecticut: $5.00 for the first report, $7.50 for each additional report within 12 months

Georgia: Two free credit reports a year

Maine: One free copy a year; $5.00 for each additional copy

Maryland: One free copy a year; $5.00 for each additional copy

Massachusetts: One free copy a year; $8.00 for each additional copy

Minnesota: $3.00 for the first report, $10.50 for each additional report within 12 months

Montana: $8.50 for each report

New Jersey: One free copy a year; $8.00 for each additional copy

U.S. Virgin Islands: $1.00 per copy

Vermont: One free copy a year; $7.50 for each additional copy

If you order your credit report by mail, you must pay with a check or money order. If you place your order by phone or online, you must pay with a major credit card.

Stay Alert for Problems

Read each of your credit reports carefully. As you will notice, the credit reports produced by Equifax, Experian, and TransUnion each have a different format and some formats are easier to read and understand than others. If you are confused about any of the information in your credit report, read the instructions that should have accompanied it. If you are still confused, call the credit reporting agency that produced the report. By law, the company must have staff available to help you understand your report.

As you review each of your credit reports, be alert for the following types of errors:

- Information that doesn't apply to you.

- Inaccurate information about your accounts. For example, although you have always paid your accounts on time, your credit history shows that you were late three times with your payments on one of your accounts.

- Out-of-date information. For example, after you fell behind on your income taxes, the IRS put a lien on your home, but a year later you paid off that debt and the lien was removed. Even so, your credit history shows that there is still a lien on your home.

- Accounts that you closed are still being reported as open.

- Information that is older than seven years is still being reported. (However, bankruptcies can be reported for up to 10 years, unpaid tax liens can be reported for up to 15 years, and court judgments can remain in your credit history for as long as 20 years.)

- Inquiries that are older than two years are being reported.

- Information that you thought had been removed from your credit record as a result of an investigation has reappeared.

Exhibit 5.1   Your Credit Reporting Legal Rights

The FCRA and the laws that have amended it give you a variety of important rights when it comes to your credit record. These laws also require credit reporting agencies, the creditors who supply information to them to as well as users of that information to do and not do certain things. If you believe that your legal rights have been

Exhibit 5.1 Continued

violated, schedule an appointment with a consumer law attorney who has specific experience handling such problems. The National Association of Consumer Advocates (NACA) at (202) 452-1989 or at www.naca.net is a good resource for finding a qualified consumer law attorney in your area. If the attorney feels that you have a strong case, you will typically not have to pay any money up-front to be represented.

You have the right to:

- Request and receive a free annual copy of your credit report from each of three national credit bureaus. This right was established by FACTA.

You can also obtain your free reports from Equifax, Experian, and TransUnion by contacting just one web site, phone number, or address. To order, visit *www.annualcreditreport.com* or *www.ftc.gov/credit*. You can call (877) 322-8228 and have the form mailed to you.

- Receive a free copy of your credit report from each of the national credit bureaus if you are unemployed and intend to apply for employment within the next 60 days. You are also entitled to a free report if you are the victim of identiy theft, or if a collection agency has told you that it reported negative information about you to a credit bureau, or may do so.

- Obtain a free copy of your credit report from the credit reporting agency that produced the report if you are denied credit, insurance, employment or a promotion

(continued)

Exhibit 5.1 Continued

because of negative information in the report. However, you must request your free report within 60 days of being notified of the denial. The creditor, insurance agency, or employer who turns you down because of your credit record information must provide you with the name and address of the credit reporting agency that provided it with your report. You are also entitled to a free report if your employer demotes or fires you in whole or in part because of your credit record information, or if your insurance company or a creditor takes an adverse action against you for the same reason. For example, the insurance company raises the cost of your premium or a creditor reduces your credit limit or raises your interest rate. Again, you must request your free report withing 60 days of being notified of the action for the report to be free. In addition, you are entitled to a free credit report if you are the victim of fraud, including identity theft.

- Have inaccurate and out-of-date credit information corrected or removed as appropriate, assuming that the credit bureau reporting the information conducts an investigation and confirms that the information is inaccurate or out-of-date.

- Have a credit bureau that corrects your credit record as a result of an investigation notify any employers who reviewed your credit history during the previous two years, or anyone else who may have looked at it over the past six months. However, you must request that

Exhibit 5.1 Continued

the employers be notified and you must provide the credit reporting agency with their names and addresses.

- Prepare a written statement of 100 words or less and have it added to your credit history when a credit bureau's investigation does not correct a problem in your credit file. In your statement, you can explain why you believe that your credit history is inaccurate. The credit reporting agency must make the statement a part of your credit file so that anyone who reviews it can read the statement. However, given that computers not humans review most credit files these days, written statements are of little use. Furthermore, they can hurt your chances of modifying your credit report later.

- File a lawsuit against a credit bureau, a business that provides information about you to a credit bureau or a business that uses your credit record information under certain circumstances, if the business willfully or negligently violates your FCRA rights.

As you learned in Exhibit 5.1, the FCRA entitles you to get inaccurate and out-of-date credit record information corrected or deleted, depending on the nature of the problem. However, doing so can be easier said than done. That's because among other reasons, credit reporting agencies don't necessarily conduct thorough investigations and if one of them investigates a problem in your credit history and concludes that the information is accurate, getting the credit reporting agency to change its mind can be an uphill battle. Even so, here is an overview of the investigation process:

1. If there is a problem in your credit record and you received a copy of it in the mail, complete the investigation request form that should have come with it. After you fill out the form, make a copy for your files and send it to the appropriate address via certified mail with a return receipt requested. If a form did not come with your credit report, your report should provide a phone number to call to initiate an investigation. If you ordered your credit report online, go to the credit reporting agency's web site and follow the directions for requesting an investigation.

If you have any information that you think will help prove the problem in your credit record—a cancelled check, a letter, a legal document, or a billing statement for example—make copies and attach them to your completed investigation request form.

2. Once the credit bureau receives your request for an investigation, it must complete its investigation within 30 days. As part of its investigation, the credit reporting agency is required to contact the provider of the information you think is incorrect within five days. The provider must certify whether or not the information is accurate.

3. If the credit bureau determines that you are correct—the information you asked to have investigated is in error or is out-of-date—it must correct the problem immediately. If the credit bureau can't confirm within the 30-day investigation period whether or not the information is

accurate, the information must be removed from your credit record. Within five days of making a correction, the credit-reporting agency must send you:

- A corrected copy of your credit report.

- A written explanation of the process it used to conduct its investigation, including the name and address of the creditor it contacted during its investigation.

- A notice informing you of your right to have the credit bureau send a corrected copy of your credit report to any employers who reviewed your credit report over the past two years and to anyone else who reviewed it over the past six months (or over the past 12 months if you live in Maryland, New York, or Vermont).

Warning A credit reporting agency can refuse to conduct an investigation if it believes that your request is frivolous or irrelevant. It must inform you in writing of its decision not to investigate and explain why it won't. It must also tell you what information you must provide in order for the credit bureau to be willing to investigate.

If an Investigation Does Not Correct Your Problem

If a credit reporting agency's investigation does not resolve the problem in your credit record, you have several options. You can:

- Provide the agency with additional information that helps document the problem.

- Contact the provider of the information you believe is inaccurate. If the provider agrees that the information

153

it supplied to the credit bureau is incorrect, ask it to report the correct information to the credit bureau and to change the information in its own database.

- Prepare a written statement for the credit bureau of no more than 100 words explaining why you believe that your credit record is in error. It will become a part of your credit record.

 Warning

As has already been noted, there is little value in written statements these days because a growing number of creditors use credit scores to evaluate consumers rather than reviewing consumers' actual credit histories. Therefore, when you apply for credit, insurance, and so on, you may want to provide the business with a copy of your written statement.

- Meet with a consumer law attorney who has specific experience resolving credit record problems. The attorney may be able to get results from the credit bureau simply by writing it a letter, or the attorney may recommend that you sue the credit reporting agency. However, for you to have a strong legal case, your lawyer must be able to prove to the court that you were harmed by the inaccuracy in your credit file.

You should also file a complaint with the Federal Trade Commission (FTC), the agency that is charged with enforcing the FCRA, and with your state attorney general's consumer protection office, if your state has its own credit reporting law (see Exhibit 5.2). To file an online complaint
(text continues on p.162)

154

Exhibit 5.2   The Fair and Accurate Credit Transaction Act of 2003

The Fair and Accurate Credit Transaction Act of 2003 (FACTA) added new sections to the federal Fair Credit Reporting Act (FCRA), intended primarily to help consumers battle the expanding crime of identity theft. Accuracy, privacy, limits on information sharing, and new consumer rights to disclosure are included in FACTA. Consumers spend an average of 175 hours cleaning up their lives after their identity has been stolen. Approximately 1 in 20 U.S. adults can expect to become a victim of identity theft, bringing the total cost to $54 billion.

Identity Theft

Fraud Alerts and Active Duty Alerts

If you are the victim of identity theft, FACTA provides you with the right to contact a credit reporting agency to identify your account. To place a *fraud alert*, you must give proof of your identity to the credit bureau. The fraud alert is initially effective for 90 days, but it may be prolonged at your request for seven years when you furnish a police report that proves to the credit bureaus that you are a victim of identity theft.

FACTA generates a different and more useful alert, an *active duty alert*, which permits active duty military personnel to place a notation on their credit report as a way to point out to potential creditors the possibility of fraud. While on duty outside the country, military members are especially open to identity theft and don't have the means

(continued)

155

Exhibit 5.2   Continued

to monitor credit activity. An active duty alert is kept in the file for at least 12 months.

If a fraud alert or active duty alert is notated on your credit report, all businesses that are asked to extend credit to you must contact you at a telephone number you provide or must take other "reasonable steps" to make certain that the credit application was not created by someone out to steal your identity.

A free copy of your credit report, under the rules of FACTA, will be provided to you when you place a fraud alert. With the extended alert (seven years), you can ask for two free copies of your report during the 12-month period after you place the alert.

You can also block certain items under the new FACTA provisions that are a result of identity theft. Similar to the fraud alert, *blocking* was already available to consumers in some states; now Congress has made it a national standard under FACTA.

Information Available to Victims

For identity theft victims, getting copies of the thief's account application and transactions is a consequential step toward regaining financial health. A business that gives credit or products and services to someone who illegally uses your identity must provide you with copies of such documents as applications for credit and transaction records. The business is also required to provide copies of documents to any federal, state, or local law enforcement agency you specify.

Exhibit 5.2   Continued

To obtain account documentation, you must supply proof of your identity. The business may also ask you to hand over a police report and an identity theft affidavit. For a copy of the Federal Trade Commission (FTC)'s fraud affidavit, visit www.ftc.gov/ bcp/edu/resources/forms/affidavit.pdf on the Internet.

Collection Agencies and Identity Theft

If you receive a call from a collection agency when you know that you have paid your bills or have not extended credit, this is usually the first sign of a problem for an identity theft victim. Under FACTA, if you are contacted by a collection agency about a debt that resulted from the theft of your identity, the collector must make certain to inform the creditor. You have the right to receive all information about this debt, such as applications, account statements, and late notices from the creditor. FACTA also says that a creditor, once notified that the debt is the work of an identity thief, cannot sell the debt or place it for collection.

How Businesses Can Prevent Identity Theft

Under the new rules, businesses that utilize credit reports must prepare a plan to detect, prevent, and mitigate identity theft. People can do only so much to protect against identity theft, because the problems mostly lie with loose procedures of credit issuers and other companies that use information from credit reports. An atmosphere of quick and easy credit has allowed some credit

(continued)

157

Exhibit 5.2 Continued

issuers to become lax when it comes to accepting a change of address, a request for a replacement credit card, or reactivation of a dormant account.

Congress understood that consumers were at a disadvantage to prevent identity theft if businesses did not pay attention to the events that signal a possible fraud. As a result, FACTA contains a plethora of stipulations that require financial institutions, creditors, and other businesses that rely on consumer credit reports to detect and resolve fraud by identity theft. They include:

- Red Flag Guidelines and requirements for credit and debit card issuers to assess the validity of a change of address request.

- Procedures to resolve different consumer addresses.

- Consumer's notation on a credit report, such as a fraud alert, active duty alert, or credit freeze.

- Peculiar patterns in the consumer's use of credit, such as a recent increase in inquiries or new credit accounts, changes in the use of credit, or accounts closed.

- Questionable documents that appear to be altered, forged, or reassembled; or documents that include information that is inconsistent with the person applying for credit.

- Suspicious Social Security number (SSN), for example, an SSN that has not been issued, that is listed on the Social Security Administration's Death Master File, that does not match the SSN range for the date of birth, or that is the same SSN as provided by other people opening accounts.

Exhibit 5.2 Continued

- Unusual address or phone number: (1) The address or phone number is known to have been furnished on fraudulent applications; (2) the address either does not exist or is that of a mail drop or prison; (3) the phone number is invalid or is associated with a pager or answering service; or (4) the address or phone number is the same as or similar to information submitted by other people opening accounts.

- Use of an account that has been inactive for a "reasonably lengthy period of time."

- Mail sent to the account holder is returned while transactions continue.

- Notice from the account holder or from law enforcement that identity theft has occurred.

Disposal of Consumer Credit Reports

The practice known as *dumpster diving* furnishes identity thieves with an abundance of personal data. Businesses that are not responsible when it comes to disposing of information have been the cause of many instances of fraud. Now under new FACTA provisions, consumer credit reporting agencies and any business that uses a consumer credit report must create procedures for proper document disposal.

The Federal Trade Commission (FTC), the federal banking agencies, and the National Credit Union Administration (NCUA) have published final regulations to implement the FACTA disposal rule. The FTC's disposal rule applies to credit reporting agencies as well as to individuals and any size

(continued)

159

Exhibit 5.2 Continued

business that uses consumer credit reports. The FTC lists the following as among those that must comply with the disposal rule:

- Lenders
- Insurers
- Employers
- Landlords
- Government agencies
- Mortgage brokers
- Automobile dealers
- Attorneys and private investigators
- Debt collectors
- Individuals who obtain a credit report on prospective nannies, contractors, or tenants
- Entities that maintain information in consumer credit reports as part of their role as service providers to other organizations covered by the rule

Notice of Consumer Rights

It is now necessary for credit reporting agencies to give identity theft victims a notice of their rights. This includes, among other things, notice of (1) the right to file a fraud alert, (2) the right to block information in a report that resulted from fraud, and (3) the right to obtain copies of documents used to commit fraud.

Exhibit 5.2 Continued

This new notice of rights supplements a general notice of rights already required by earlier FCRA amendments. The FTC has circulated final regulations and a sample copy of the identity theft rights. Under the FTC's rule, consumers who report fraud to a consumer credit reporting agency will receive the special victims' notice of rights. The FTC's final rule also contains notices that clarify the obligations of companies that provide information on consumers as well as those that use consumer credit reports.

Negative Information in a Consumer Credit Report Due to Identity Theft

The most important element for detecting identity theft is to check your credit report regularly. False information about late payments and collection actions is what you don't want to see. But catching fraud early enables you to more quickly regain your financial health.

FACTA now requires creditors to supply you with what might be called an "early warning" notice. This notice could alert you that something is wrong with an account. Don't take this notice for granted. You should still check your credit reports, bank accounts, and credit card statements on your own. Be diligent, and be wary! You may have to look closely to even see this new notice among the other entries.

A financial institution that extends credit must send you a notice no later than 30 days after negative information is furnished to a credit bureau. *Negative information* includes late payments, missed payments, partial payments, or any other form of default on the account.

(continued)

Exhibit 5.2 Continued

You should not be lax and feel that you are secure just because a creditor is obligated to send you a notice before posting negative information to your credit report. Identity thieves are devious and creative. They are bold enough and deceptive enough to take over your existing accounts. And they might open new accounts right under your nose. Your best defense against fraud is always to review your credit reports as well as your monthly credit card and bank account statements.

Information Sharing among Affiliates— Opt Out for Marketing

With the new FACTA rules, you will be given a chance to *opt out*, that is, halt a corporation's affiliates from sharing customer data for marketing purposes. This opt-out is an extra component to the existing opt-out choices for information shared with third-party nonaffiliates and an existing opt out under the FCRA.

---

with the FTC, go to www.ftc.gov. You can also call (800) 382-4357 or mail your complaint to the Federal Trade Commission, Consumer Response Center, 600 Pennsylvania Ave., NW, Washington, DC 20580. Be as specific as possible in your complaint and provide all applicable dates and backup information.

How Do You Score?

A growing number of creditors and insurance companies are using consumers' credit scores rather than reviewing their credit record information in order to make decisions about them. Your credit score is derived from your credit history information and it is a numerical representation of how well you have managed your credit in the past and how well you are likely to manage it in the future. Your credit score will probably range from 300 to 850. The higher your credit score the better, although a score of 720 and over is considered a very good score.

A low credit score, like a credit history full of negative information, can have many negative effects on your life. It may cause:

- You to be denied credit, insurance, or employment.

- The terms of your existing credit accounts may be changed. For example, your credit limits may be lowered, your interest rates may be increased, and so on.

- The cost of your insurance premium may go up.

Fair, Isaac, Inc. is the main provider of credit scores to financial institutions and other creditors. Its score is referred to as the *FICO score,* a term that has become virtually synonymous with credit scores. However, some companies generate their own credit scores. For example, the Equifax credit score is known as BEACON; Experian's is called the Experian/Fair Isaac Risk score; and TransUnion's credit score is called EMPIRICA. Fair, Isaac helped each of the three national credit-reporting agencies develop their credit scores.

Your credit score is derived by applying a mathematical formula to your credit record information. Other information may also be taken into account including your income, employment history, whether or not you own your home, and so on. Also, different credit scoring formulas may not give the same weight to your information, which means that your credit score will vary depending on who generates it.

Warning   Your credit score will be harmed if you are close to your credit limit on any of your accounts.

Here are the approximate weights that Fair Isaac will give to your information when it calculates your FICA score:

Your account payment history   35%
(Fair, Isaac will place the greatest emphasis on your most recent account payment history.)

Your total amount of debt and the total amount of   30%
credit that is available to you

How long you have had credit   15%
(Having had credit for a long time will help your credit score, especially if you have had credit with the same creditors for many years.)

Types of credit   10%
(Having a healthy mix of different types of credit—installment loans, credit cards, a mortgage, etc.—will help your score. However, don't go out and get new credit just to be more diversified.)

Amount of new credit you are applying for   10%
(Applying for a lot of credit within a relatively short period of time will hurt your credit score, especially if you have been late recently with your payments,

are over your credit limit on some of your cards, or if any of your accounts have been sent to collections.)

 Warning Transferring a balance from a long standing credit card to a new card and then closing the account that you transferred the balance from may harm your score because you will have lowered the average age of your accounts.

How to Order Your Credit Score

To order your FICO score from Fair, Isaac, go to www .myfico.com. If you want to purchase your credit score from the three national credit bureaus, you can buy them at the Fair, Isaac web site. You can also purchase them directly from each of the three national credit reporting agencies by mail, phone or at their web sites.

How to Raise Your Credit Score

Is your credit score below par? Follow this common sense advice to increase it:

- Don't have a lot of credit cards, even if all of them have low or zero balances.

- Keep your credit card balances to a minimum. Being close to or at a credit limit will harm your score.

- If you have a lot of credit card debt, work at paying it off rather than by transferring it to a lower interest card. The danger with transfers is that you may come close to or reach your credit limit on the card that you transfer your balances to.

- Pay your debts on time.

- Don't close long-standing credit card accounts.

- Maintain a checking account as well as a savings account.

- Don't apply for a lot of credit. The more often you apply for credit, the more inquiries there will be in your credit file. Having a lot of inquiries will lower your score substantially.

- Be especially careful when shopping for a new car. Car dealerships are notorious for pulling customers' credit reports without their knowledge. Remember, the more credit-related inquiries related to you, the lower your score.

Warning

Surfing the Net for the best rate on a loan can lower your credit score because each time you ask for an interest rate quote, the lender will run a credit check and each credit check will show up in your credit file as an inquiry.

- Resist offers to apply for a store's own credit card, even if the store offers you an on-the-spot discount on your purchases as an enticement to take the card or offers you some other benefit. Each time you apply for one of these cards a new inquiry will be added to your credit file. On top of that, new accounts will bring down the average age of all of your accounts, which in turn will lower your credit score.

- When you are in the market for a mortgage or a car loan, shop for the best deal within a relatively short period of time. When you do, Fair Isaac Corporation will distinguish between shopping for a single loan and shopping for a lot of credit. Therefore, your credit score will not be harmed.

- Maintain a positive credit history, review it once every six months and when you find problems, get them corrected as quickly as possible.

- If you have damaged your credit history, open some new accounts, pay them on time, and don't run up your account balances. Over time, your credit score will improve.

167

Chapter SIX

Rebuilding Your Credit History and Your Financial Future

Annette is able to see the light at the end of the tunnel after a difficult couple of years. After losing her job of four years, Annette depleted her savings account to pay her bills while she looked for new employment. Eventually, Annette took a job that paid her less than she had been earning. Also because her new job did not provide her with any health care benefits, Annette purchased a high deductible health insurance policy. Then, disaster struck. Annette became ill and was hospitalized for two days. When she left the hospital she owed a substantial amount of money. Although she worked out a plan for paying the hospital what she owed over time, the payments put an even bigger strain on Annette's finances and she fell behind on some of her bills. Eventually, however, with the help of a nonprofit debt counseling agency and a lot of sacrifice on Annette's part, she got out of debt. Now, Annette is financially stable again and is earning good money, but her credit history is damaged. Therefore, she has begun the credit rebuilding process because she wants to buy a home someday. However, Annette realizes that

*it will take time to rebuild her credit and that there are no short
cuts. Therefore, she is committed to doing it one step at a time,
little by little.*

W hen you live on a cash-only basis, it's easy to stay
out of financial trouble because you can only buy
what you have the money for. However, in our society, you need access to credit in order to purchase big-
ticket items like the house Annette wants to buy or to rent
a car and reserve a hotel room, and to shop online, among
other things. Plus, having credit makes life easier. Having
access to credit is a wonderful convenience, assuming you
manage it responsibly.

Hopefully, if you have been in financial trouble and
you have been following the advice in this book, you have
learned how to manage your finances responsibly and your
financial situation has begun to improve. If so, you are in
the same situation as Annette—ready to begin rebuilding
your credit history. This chapter tells you how to do that
step by step.

Proving That You Are Worthy of Credit Again

When you have been to Credit Hell and back, you face the
challenge of proving to creditors that your financial problems are behind you and that if they give you new credit,
you will manage it responsibly. However, creditors will not
simply take your word for it. You will have to demonstrate
through your actions over time that you are creditworthy
again. Remember, too, negative credit record information
will remain in your credit history for at least seven years, so

you will be stuck with that information for a while. Only time will make it go away. Even so, once your financial troubles are behind you, you should begin adding positive information to your credit record and, eventually, as the old negative information gets dropped from your credit file, you will end up with a good credit record, assuming that everything you add to your credit history is positive.

Tip

If your credit problems damaged but did not destroy your credit history and if you have been making on-time payments to your creditors for six months or longer, write to them to inquire as to whether they are willing to remove the old information from your credit file. Explain what caused you to get into trouble and point out your recent positive payment history, as well as the length of time that you have been doing business with them (as long as it is more than one year).

Step 1: Build Up Your Savings

If you have not already begun a regular program of savings, it's time to start. Although you should try to save as much as you can, how much you save each month is less important than getting into the habit of regular contributions to your savings account. Shop around for the best interest rate so your money will grow as fast as possible. Remember, however, a savings account is not meant to be invaded.

As I explained in the very first chapter of this book, it's essential that you have enough money in a savings or money market account that if you lost your job tomorrow,

170

you could continue paying your bills for the next six to nine months. You need additional funds in your savings account as well just in case you are hit with an unexpected emergency. Another reason to build up your savings is that at the start of the rebuilding process you may not be able to qualify for a regular credit card so you will have to apply for a secured card instead. Also, when you have money in a savings or money market account, creditors are more apt to see you as a financially stable person and a good credit risk.

Step 2: Review Your Credit History

Order a copy of your credit history from each of the three national credit reporting agencies—Equifax, Experian, and TransUnion—and review each report for accuracy. If you find any inaccuracies, get them corrected. You do not want an error in any of your credit records to derail your rebuilding effort. Chapter 5 explains how to order your credit reports by phone, in writing, or at the web sites of each agency, highlights problems to look for; and explains how to correct any problems you may find.

If you have any positive account information that is not in your credit records, you can provide it to the credit reporting agencies and ask that it be added. However, they are not legally obligated to add it. Put your request in writing. However, don't be disappointed if the information does not show up in your credit reports.

Step 3: Apply for a MasterCard or Visa

Once you have $500 to $1,000 in a savings or money market account and after you have addressed any errors in your credit history, apply for a MasterCard or Visa. Apply for the one with the best terms of credit. (Chapter 4 discussed how to evaluate credit card offers.)

If it is possible given your recent financial problems that you won't be able to qualify for a regular MasterCard or Visa. Instead, you may have to apply for a secured credit card, which will look exactly like a regular MasterCard or Visa. However, a secured card works differently. To use a secured card, you must put a certain amount of money in a savings account or purchase a certificate of deposit (CD) for a certain amount of money from the bank that issues you the card. The money or CD will collateralize your credit card purchases and you will only be able to charge up to a certain percentage of the value of your collateral. For example, if you secure the card with $1,000, you might be able to charge up to $750, depending on the terms of the card. Then, if you don't make your card payments according to the terms of your credit agreement, the card issuer can get paid by tapping your collateral. In addition to losing some or all of your collateral when you don't live up to the terms of the agreement, you will also undermine your credit rebuilding efforts because the creditor may report that information to the credit bureau(s) it works with. However, the opposite will be true if you make your payments on time, do not exceed your credit limit, and so on. As a result, you will probably qualify for a regular Master-Card or Visa eventually.

Warning Secured credit card issuers are notorious for charging their cardholders excessive penalties and fees for various services. These charges add up over time. Therefore, evaluate each secured card offer carefully to make certain that you won't be overcharged.

You should shop for a secured card as carefully as you would shop for a regular MasterCard or Visa. However, when you are comparing secured card offers, you will have a few additional criteria to consider in addition to the credit card criteria outlined in Chapter 4. For example, when you are evaluating a secured card you should also take into account:

- How much money do you need in a savings account or how big a CD do you need to purchase and what interest rate will apply to the account or CD?

- Can you increase your credit limit? If you can, how long will you have to wait to get the increase and will you have to increase your collateral?

- Will the card issuer report your payments to one or more of the national credit reporting agencies? There is no point in applying for a secured card from a card issuer who will not report your payments since the card will do nothing to help rebuild your credit history.

Warning Steer clear of secured cards issued by firms that do not report to the national credit reporting agencies and that tend to come with especially unattractive terms of credit. Also secured card offerings associated with an insurance policy of some sort almost always come with very high fees. Beware.

When is the card issuer entitled to take your collateral?

- Will the secured card convert to an unsecured card eventually? Under what circumstances? Will you have to pay a conversion fee?

> Convert to an unsecured card as soon as you can since most secured cards come with higher rates of interest than unsecured cards and because your collateral may not be earning a competitive rate of interest.

- If you can convert, what interest rate and conditions will apply to the unsecured card? If they are not attractive, shop for an unsecured card with better terms of credit once you have established a record of on-time payments on your secured card, or its converted equivalent.

- If you close your secured card account, can you get your collateral back? What conditions will apply and how long will it take to get your money back?

Once you have a secured card, use it one of two ways to rebuild your credit history. One alternative is to use the card to purchase something that does not cost a lot and then pay your account balance in full once you receive your account statement. Then, you should purchase something else with the card, pay that balance in full, and so on. Or, you can use your card to make a large purchase then pay off your card balance over time. However, by now you should realize that the latter option should not be your first choice and should be avoided. Either way, you should realize, assuming you are not late with your payments, you will begin adding new positive information to your credit record and eventually, you will qualify for an unsecured MasterCard or Visa with reasonable terms.

Step 4: Get a Bank Loan

Part of the credit rebuilding process also involves getting a small bank loan—between $500 and $1,000—and repaying it according to the terms of your loan agreement. You will need additional funds in a savings or money market account to collateralize the loan since it is unlikely that a bank will give you an unsecured loan, even for such a small amount. Please note, you will not be able to use the funds that are securing your MasterCard or Visa to secure the loan.

Contact a loan officer with the bank where you have your savings account now. Let the officer know that you have begun the credit rebuilding process after having financial problems and you would like to borrow a small amount of money from the bank as part of that process. Be prepared to explain what led to your problems and what you have done to ensure that they won't reoccur.

If the loan officer is not interested in working with you because of your credit history or if your loan application is denied, contact a loan officer with another bank. Eventually, you will find a bank that is willing to work with you. If none of the banks in your area is willing to give you a loan, then bide your time, continue to manage your finances responsibly, pay your secured credit card on time, and continue depositing money into savings.

175

Eventually, you will have put enough distance between you and your past money troubles and you will have added enough positive information to your credit record that you will be able to find a lender who will make you a loan. Once you do, pay your loan on time and in accordance with its terms.

After you have paid off your secured loan, apply for a small, unsecured loan. Apply first to the bank that made you the first loan. If that bank denies your application, shop around to see if there is a lender in your area that will loan you money and find out the kinds of terms that will apply to the loan. If more than one lender is willing to work with you, go with the bank that offers you the best terms of credit.

When you apply for a bank loan always try to meet in person with a loan officer. It is important that you have an opportunity to thoroughly explain why your credit is bad and to remind this person of your timely debt payments since. You want the loan officer to consider this information when he or she is deciding whether or not to give you a loan.

If you can't qualify for an unsecured loan, then apply for another secured loan. Depending on how badly your credit history was damaged and the strength of your current financial situation, it may take time before any bank will loan you money on an unsecured basis, but it will happen eventually as long as you continue to manage your finances responsibly.

Before you apply for your second bank loan, order a copy of your credit report from each of the three national credit reporting agencies. Make sure that the payments you made on your first loan were reported accurately and review your credit history for potential problems. If the new loans and your successful liquidation of them are not reported, contact the lender and ask that they be reported. Also, if there are any errors in your credit history, correct them before you apply for a new loan.

Chapter SEVEN

Your Money Rights

Wade T. was being hounded by debt collectors about several past due debts. They called him so often at home and at work that he didn't want to answer his phone for fear a debt collector would be on the other end of the line. One debt collector had warned Wade that he could end up in jail if he did not pay what he owed. That comment really scared Wade because he did not have the money to pay the debt collectors and they just wouldn't take "no" for an answer. Wade did not want to ask his parents for help because he was embarrassed that he had gotten himself into so much financial trouble. Wade thought his only option was to pay off the debts using some of the cash advance checks two of his credit card companies sent him every month even though he knew that the last thing he needed was more debt. However, he just wanted to get the debt collectors off his back!

It's too bad that Wade did not know about a federal law called the Fair Debt Collection Practices Act. If he did, Wade would have known that the debt collector who threatened him with jail time was breaking the law and that he was entitled to tell all of the debt collectors to stop calling him. However, like most consumers, Wade was unaware of the laws that have been passed to protect consumers when they apply for and use credit, find problems in their credit records, or fall behind on their bills. Yet, knowing about those laws and understanding how to use them is an important part of avoiding problems when you use credit, maintaining a problem-free credit record, and staying out of Credit Hell. The information will also help you get your money's worth when you purchase goods and services with a credit card, resolve problems in your financial life as quickly and cheaply as possible, and manage your finances responsibly. Too often, however, consumers don't learn about the laws that can protect them until they have been ripped off, had their lives made miserable by debt collectors, been turned down for credit because of inaccurate information in their credit files, or been harmed in some other way. This chapter increases your legal IQ by providing you with basic information about the key federal consumer protection laws. It also educates you about your options when you believe that your legal rights have been violated.

 Your state may have its own laws similar to the federal laws discussed in this chapter. Your state's laws may provide you with more protection than their federal counterparts. Call your state attorney general's office of consumer protection or visit its web site to find out about the consumer protection laws in your state.

Your Legal Rights When You Use Credit and Owe Money

There are many federal laws that protect you when you apply for and use credit. They include the Truth in Lending Act, the Equal Credit Opportunity Act, the Home Equity Loan Consumer Protection Act, the Fair Credit Billing Act, and the Credit Practices Rule, among others. Two other important laws apply when you have fallen behind on your debts. They are the Fair Debt Collection Practices Act and the Federal Bankruptcy Code. Chapter 2 explained how bankruptcy works. This chapter also discusses other consumer laws you should know about, including the Credit Repair Organizations Act and the Electronic Fund Transfer Act. Another very important law, the Fair Credit Practices Act was discussed in detail in Chapter 5.

Laws That Protect You When You Apply for Credit

The Equal Credit Opportunity Act (ECOA), the Truth in Lending Act (TILA), and the Home Equity Loan Consumer Protection Act give you specific rights when you apply for credit and require creditors to provide you with specific information. For information about your TILA rights, return to Chapter 4.

The Equal Credit Opportunity Act: The federal Equal Credit Opportunity Act (ECOA) prohibits creditors from discriminating against you when you apply for credit, including credit cards and bank loans, because of your gender, age, race, national origin, religion, marital status, or because you are receiving public assistance. This law applies to any business that grants credit to consumers, including banks, finance companies, retail and department stores, credit card companies, and credit unions.

Tip Some aspects of the ECOA protect you when you use credit.

Among other things, the ECOA says that when you apply for credit, creditors cannot:

- Ask you about your gender, race, national origin, or religion, although they can ask you about this information when you apply for a real estate loan. However, you don't have to answer their questions. The information will be used by the federal government for statistical purposes.

- Discriminate against you on the basis of your age. However, creditors can consider your age relative to other factors they may use to assess your creditworthiness. For example, if you are close to retirement age, they could consider the fact that your income may drop once you are retired.

- Give you less credit or credit with less favorable terms than what they would give someone else with your same financial information because of your gender, age, race, national origin, religion, marital status, or because you are receiving public assistance.

- Ask you about your marital status if you apply for individual, unsecured credit. However, if you live in a community property state (Arizona, California, Idaho, Louisiana, Nevada, New Mexico, Texas, and Washington state), creditors can ask you about your marital status when you apply for joint credit or individual secured credit.

- Take into account whether or not you have a telephone listed in your name. However, creditors can consider whether or not you have a phone.

- Consider the race of people in the neighborhood when you want to borrow money to buy a home, refinance an existing mortgage, or remodel your home.

- Discount your income because of your gender or marital status. For example, if you are a woman and you earn $40,000/year, a creditor cannot consider only a fraction of your total income—75 percent, for example—when evaluating your credit application but consider 100 percent of your male coworker's $40,000 salary when he applies for the same credit.

- Discount or refuse to consider income you may earn from a part-time job, a pension, an annuity, or from a retirement benefits program.

Women get special protection from the ECOA: The ECOA gives married women special rights and protections in order to help them establish their own credit histories separate from their spouses' and so they can open credit accounts in their own names. These special rights help protect women against the financial repercussions of divorce or widowhood because without their own credit accounts and credit

182

history, they are likely to face an uphill battle when they are trying to rebuild their lives.

If you are married, the ECOA gives you the right to:

- Get credit in your maiden name, your first name and your spouse's last name, or use a hyphenated last name that is a combination of your first and last names and your spouse's last name (e.g., Jane Smith-Nichols).

- Have your credit application evaluated according to your own income and credit history.

- Have all of your income considered during the credit application process, including regular income from part-time work, public assistance, alimony or maintenance, and child support. However, creditors can require you to prove the reliability of such income.

- Obtain credit without a cosigner, assuming you qualify on your own for the credit.

- Have someone other than your spouse cosign a credit agreement, if you need a cosigner. However, if you apply for secured credit and you live in a community property state, creditors are entitled to require your spouse to cosign for the credit even if you qualify for it on your own. They can also require that your spouse sign the ownership documents for purchases like real estate or a car.

- Maintain your own credit accounts after you change your name, your marital status, reach a certain age, or retire, unless the creditor has evidence that you cannot afford to continue paying on the accounts.

If you already have credit in your own name, don't close those accounts when you get married. Continue to maintain them in your own name. There is no law requiring you to merge your credit identity with your spouse's. You need your own credit and your own credit history totally separate from your spouse's because you don't know what your future will bring and you need to be prepared financially. Furthermore, if your future spouse has a questionable credit history or if he gets one after you are married, when you merge your credit with his, your credit history will also be negatively affected.

The ECOA also says that creditors cannot ask you:

- For information about your spouse, unless your spouse is your co-applicant, your spouse will be an authorized user on your account, you are relying on your spouse's income to qualify for the credit, or unless you live in a community property state.

- About your plans to have children or about your method of birth control. Creditors are also prohibited from assuming that if you are of child-bearing age, you will stop working to raise a family.

To help you build your own credit history, the ECOA requires creditors to report information about the credit accounts you share with your spouse in your name as well as in your spouse's.

What the ECOA requires after you have applied for credit: The ECOA says that after you apply for credit, the creditor must tell you in writing within 30 days whether your credit application has been approved. If it is denied, the creditor must provide you with specific written reasons for the denial or must tell you how to get that information. Possible reasons include you don't have enough income, you have been late paying some of your creditors, your credit score is low, you do not have a long enough employment history, and so on.

The creditor must also give you the name, address, and phone number of the credit reporting agency that provided it with your credit record information during its application review process. If you contact that credit bureau within 60 days of receiving the creditor's denial notice, you are entitled to a free copy of your credit report. Otherwise, you must pay for it. Chapter 5 tells you how to order your credit report.

Warning

If a creditor says that you must contact it to find out why your credit application was denied, you must do so within 60 days. Otherwise, the creditor is not obligated to provide you with the information.

If you are approved for credit but at less favorable terms than you applied for, the ECOA entitles you to find out why, unless you accept the terms you were offered. Less favorable terms of credit could include a higher interest rate, a lower credit limit, a smaller loan amount, a smaller credit line, and so on. Again, be sure to contact the creditor within 60 days of receiving the creditor's response to your application.

The Home Equity Loan Consumer Protection Act

The Home Equity Loan Consumer Protection Act (HEL-CPA) says that lenders must give you certain written information when you apply for a home equity loan or a home equity line of credit. That information includes:

- The rate(s) and fees that apply to the credit.

- A warning that you may lose your home if you do not meet the terms of the credit.

- The amount of any balloon payments you may have to pay.

- Which terms of credit may be subject to change.

- The fact that you have the right of *recession,* which gives you an opportunity to change your mind about borrowing against the equity in your home during a three-day cooling-off period. This period ends at midnight on the third business day after you have received the HELCPA-required information. By the way, Saturday is considered a business day. To take advantage of this right, you must notify the lender in writing or via a telegram of your change of heart. Once the lender receives your cancellation notice, it has 20 days to return any money it has received from you and to release any security interest it has in your home.

The Fair Credit Billing Act

When you purchase goods or services with a bankcard or a retail store charge card and you discover an error on your account billing statement, you have the right to have the problem resolved through the dispute resolution process established by the federal Fair Credit Billing Act (FCBA). The FCBA applies to such errors as:

- Your account is not properly credited for a payment you made or for a refund you are entitled to.

- Charges that you did not authorize appear on your statement. As you learned in Chapter 4, the law limits your responsibility for these charges to $50 within certain time frames.

- You are charged the wrong amount for a purchase.

- There are mathematical errors on your account statement.

- You are billed for goods or services you did not accept or that were never delivered as agreed.

- Your account billing statement arrives late because it was sent to your former address even though you provided the creditor with written notice of your change of address at least 20 days before the end of the period you were billed for.

- Your account statement reflects charges for insurance or for another type of service or product sold by a credit card company but you did not authorize the charges.

For the FCBA to protect you, the creditor must receive a letter from you regarding an error in your account billing statement no later than 60 days after the date that the first billing statement reflecting the error was mailed to you. Therefore, as soon as you discover a problem in your billing statement, write, do not call, the creditor. Calling won't activate the protections of the FCBA.

187

In your letter, explain the nature of your account billing statement problem clearly and succinctly and note the date and amount of the error. Include your account number, your name as it appears on your account, and your billing address in the letter. Then, make a copy of the letter for your files and attach to the letter copies of any receipts, correspondence, cancelled checks, bank statements, and any other written materials you may have that help document the problem.

Mail your letter to the address on your credit card account billing statement for "billing inquiries." Do not include it with your account payment. Send the letter to the creditor via certified mail with a return receipt requested. That way you will have proof of exactly when it was received. This is important because the FCBA says that the creditor must acknowledge your letter within 30 days of receiving it unless your problem has already been resolved by then. Also, the creditor must resolve your problem one way or another within two billing cycles, but not longer than 90 days.

While the creditor is investigating your problem, you do not have to pay the amount in question or any related charges. However, you must continue paying the rest of your bill. Also, during the investigation period, the creditor cannot report to credit bureaus that your account is delinquent, although it can report that your account is in dispute, and it cannot threaten to harm your credit score. Also, while the creditor's investigation is ongoing, it cannot close your account, restrict your use of the account because of the disputed amount, or send the amount you are disputing and/or related charges to collections. However, the creditor can apply the disputed amount and related charges to your credit limit.

If, as a result of its investigation, the creditor concurs that there is an error in your account statement, he must inform you of that conclusion in writing and must let you know what he has done or will do to correct it. If the creditor credits your account, he must remove all finance charges, late fees, and other charges related to the error.

If the creditor concludes that your account statement is accurate, you must pay the amount you disputed as well as any accumulated finance charges. You may also have to pay the minimum amount you did not pay because of the dispute. The creditor is required to promptly inform you of exactly how much you owe and must provide you with a written explanation of why you owe the money. You are also entitled to ask for documentation proving what you owe.

If you disagree with the creditor's conclusion, you can let the creditor know in writing and you can also refuse to pay the disputed amount, assuming you do so within 10 days of receiving the creditor's notice informing you of his investigation results. However, at this point, the creditor is legally entitled to try to collect the money and can report to credit reporting agencies that your account is past due although it must also report that you dispute the fact that you owe the past due amount. You are entitled to know to which credit reporting agencies the creditor has reported this information.

Other Rights under the FCBA

The FCBA also says that creditors that extend open-end credit to consumers such as MasterCards and Visa card must:

- Provide you with a written explanation of your right to dispute account billing errors when you open your account.

- Provide you with a monthly billing statement for each billing period in which either you owe more than $1 on your account or you are owed at least that much by the creditor.

- Mail your billing statement to you at least 14 days before your payment due date.

- Credit your account promptly when you are owed more than $1. The same applies to refunds you may be owed. If you request a refund rather than a credit, the creditor must send it to you within seven business days after receiving your request letter.

The FCBA provides other important protections when you purchase merchandise with a credit card and the item turns out to be damaged, defective, or shoddily made or when you use your credit card to purchase a service and the service is never provided or is not provided according to the terms of your contract with the service provider. The law says that when these circumstances apply, you can take the same legal actions against the card issuer that your state law allows you to take against the seller. However, to take advantage of this protection, you must have purchased the merchandise or service in your home state or within 100 miles of your current billing address. In addition, you must have paid more than $50 for the merchandise or service and you must have already made a good faith effort to resolve your problem directly with the seller.

However, none of those caveats apply if the seller is also the card issuer. For example, you purchased goods from a retailer using the retailer's charge card.

If your efforts to resolve your problem with a friendly letter to the creditor are not successful, you are legally entitled to withhold payment. However, the creditor can try to collect the money from you.

 Warning If you purchase merchandise or services with a debit card, the federal Electronic Fund Transfer Act, not the FCBA, covers you. That law is covered later in this chapter.

The Credit Practices Rule

The Credit Practices Rule applies to consumer credit contracts, other than real estate-related contracts, offered by finance companies, auto dealers, furniture and department stores, and other types of retailers, as well as to credit unions. (It does not apply to banks, bank cards like MasterCard and Visa, or to savings and loan associations.) It says that the consumer credit contracts offered by these types of businesses cannot require you to:

- Agree in advance that should they sue you for non-payment of a debt, you will forfeit your right to be notified of any court hearings related to the lawsuit. Not being notified about such hearings would make it impossible for you to be represented by an attorney so that your side of the issue could be presented at the hearing.

191

- Give up any protections provided to you under your state's law that permit you to keep certain types of personal assets even if you do not pay your debt as agreed. This type of provision is called a *waiver of exemption.* Most states have laws that allow you to protect your home, clothing, household items, and other personal belongings up to a certain dollar value from a creditor's (or debt collector's) collection actions. However, if you used the item that you owe money on to secure the debt that you incurred to purchase the item, and then the rule does not protect you from a creditor's collection actions.

- Agree in advance that the creditor can garnish your wages if you default on your debt.

- Collateralize your debt with household or personal items that are of significant value to you but that have little or no economic value to the creditor. Such items might include your linens, china, wedding ring, family photos, personal papers, your family Bible, and your household pets, among other things. However, if you collateralized your debt using any such items, the rule allows the creditor to repossess them if you don't repay the debt according to the terms of your agreement.

The Credit Practices Rule also makes it illegal for a creditor to charge you a late fee because you haven't paid a previous late fee. This practice is called *pyramiding late fees.* In other words, if you do not include the late fee you owe with your next regular payment, the creditor cannot subtract the amount of the unpaid late fee from the amount of your payment and then charge you a second late fee because the payment you just made was insufficient as a result of the deduction. However, if you skip a payment, the creditor can charge late fees on all subsequent payments until you bring your account up-to-date.

Cosigning a Debt and the Credit Practices Rule

The Credit Practices Rule also applies when you agree to cosign someone else's debt. For example, your son just graduated from college and cannot qualify for a loan to purchase a car because he has no credit history. However, if you agree to cosign his car loan and your son defaults on the loan, the lender can look to you for the car payments. The rule requires the creditor to give you a written notice explaining:

- Your risks and responsibilities as a cosigner.

- Informing you of the fact that the creditor is legally entitled to try to collect from you whatever the borrower does not pay rather than trying to collect from the borrower. The creditor may try to collect using such methods as lawsuits and wage garnishment.

- Informing you of the fact that if the cosigned debt is ever in default, that information could end up in your credit record.

Tip

Some states require creditors to try to collect from the borrower first when he or she defaults on a cosigned debt. If the creditor is unable to collect from the borrower, the creditor can try to get its money from the cosigner.

Warning It's always best to avoid cosigning notes, no matter what your relationship with a borrower. All too often people feel compelled to be a cosigner out of fear that not agreeing will be detrimental to their relationship. However, if your relationship is truly a good one, it should survive when you say "No." This rule of thumb also applies when a loved one asks to borrow your credit card.

Your Debt Collection Rights

Owing money to creditors that you cannot afford to pay is stressful enough, but being hounded by debt collectors about your unpaid debts can make life a living hell especially if the debt collectors use threats and scare tactics to get you to pay. However, the federal Fair Debt Collection Practices Act (FDCPA) gives you important rights when you are contacted by a debt collector and sets out clear guidelines for what debt collectors can and cannot do when they are trying to collect money from you.

The FDCPA applies to personal, family, and household debts, including past due credit card debts, mortgages, car loans, student loans and other personal loans, medical and insurance debts, utility bills, condo fees, unpaid legal judgments, and bounced checks. It applies not only to debt collectors but also to attorneys who collect debts for their clients. The FDCPA does not apply to in-house debt collectors or to federal and state government employees who collect debts for government agencies.

Here is a summary of what debt collectors covered by the FDCPA *cannot do* when they are trying to collect from you:

- Call you at an inconvenient time or place such as before 8 A.M. or after 9 P.M. unless you give them permission to do so.

- Call you at work if they know that your employer does not want you to be called there. Also, they cannot contact your employer about your debt.

- Contact you by postcard or use an envelope that makes it clear that it was sent by a debt collector.

- Contact you after you have requested that you not be contacted again.

- Try to scare you into paying a debt by sending you a letter that appears to have come from a government agency or a court of law.

- Call you repeatedly within a short period of time—every hour during an afternoon, or day after day, for example.

- Contact your neighbors, relatives, friends, or other people to get information that can help them collect the money that you owe.

- Use profanity when communicating with you.

- Threaten to ruin your reputation, harm you or your property, or throw you in jail unless you pay your debt. However, debt collectors can threaten to sue you assuming they are willing to follow through on their threat.

• Order you to accept their collect calls or pay for their telegrams.

• Collect more than the amount that you owe, unless it is allowed under your state's law.

• Deposit a post-dated check before its date.

• Take your property or threaten to take it unless they are legally entitled to.

 If a debt collector is trying to collect multiple debts from you, payments you make on one debt must be applied to that particular debt. Also, the debt collector cannot apply your payment to a debt you don't believe you owe.

Within five days of contacting you for the first time about a debt, the debt collector must provide you with written information detailing exactly how much money you owe and to whom you owe it. The information must also inform you of your right to dispute the debt.

Responding to a Debt Collector

The FDCPA gives you several options for responding to a debt collector. Your best option will depend on your financial situation, the nature of the debt that the collector wants to collect, and whether or not you agree that you owe it. You can:

- Pay the debt if you agree that you owe it and assuming that you have the money to pay it, and that if you pay it, you will have the money you need to cover all of your basic living expenses and your high-priority debts. Chapter 2 explains how to distinguish between high- and low-priority debts.

 Warning Don't pay a low-priority debt just because the debt collector demands that you do so.

- Work out an affordable debt payment plan with the debt collector.

 Warning Never agree to make payments that you cannot afford just to get a debt collector off your back.

- Try to settle the debt for less than what you owe on it.
- Send the debt collector a letter within 30 days of receiving a written notice about the debt stating that you do not owe it. Once the debt collector receives your letter, it cannot contact you again about the debt except to send you proof that you owe it.
- Ask the debt collector for written verification that you owe the debt. You should do this if you are not sure that the debt collector is accurate about how much you owe or if you want to buy yourself time to figure out what to do about the debt.
- Write the debt collector to state that you do not want to be contacted again. The debt collector must comply with your request. However, he can send you a

notice confirming that it won't contact you again or informing you of a specific collection action that he intends to take.

- Dispute the debt. If you don't believe that you owe a debt or if you disagree with the amount that the debt collector says you owe, you can send the debt collector a dispute letter. You must send it within 30 days of being contacted about the debt for the first time. Once the debt collector receives your letter, he must suspend all collection efforts while it confirms the validity of the debt.

Warning It will certainly be a big relief not to receive calls and letters from a debt collector. However, stopping all communication with a debt collector won't make a debt go away, assuming you owe it. Therefore, the debt collector may take other steps to collect from you—sue you for example. Furthermore, by stopping all communication, you will have eliminated the option of settling your debt for less or negotiating an affordable debt payment plan.

- File for bankruptcy. This is your best option if you cannot afford to pay a secured debt and you want to keep the asset that collateralizes it—your home or car, for example. It's also your best option if you owe a substantial amount of unsecured debt and you either need time to repay it without pressure from creditors and debt collectors or if there is no way that you can repay what you owe.

Other Laws You Should Know About

There are three other important federal consumer laws that you should be familiar with. They are the Fair Credit Reporting Act, which was discussed in Chapter 5, the Credit Repair Organizations Act, and the Electronic Fund Transfer Act.

The Credit Repair Organizations Act

The Credit Repair Organizations Act (CROA) protects you when you work with a forprofit or nonprofit organization that provides credit rebuilding assistance. The law was enacted because disreputable credit repair organizations were victimizing consumers by taking their money and then not delivering on their promises. They were also encouraging consumers to use illegal means to rebuild their credit histories, and charging them exorbitant amounts of money for their services without letting consumers know that they could rebuild their own credit histories for little or no money. Chapter 6 explains the credit rebuilding process.

Among other things, the CROA says that a credit repair organization:

- Must give you a written contract that explains the specific services it will provide to you, their total cost, and how long it will take to achieve the promised results. The contract must also spell out what guarantees if any, the organization is making to you and provide the organization's name and address.

- Cannot take money from you or charge you in any way until it has provided you with all of the services spelled out in its contract.

- Must give you three business days to cancel the contract after you have signed it. You must use the cancellation form provided by the credit repair firm.

- Cannot provide you with any of the services you have contracted for until the end of the three-day cancellation period.

- Must give you a disclosure statement before you sign its contract. This statement must tell you that you are legally entitled to dispute inaccurate or out-of-date credit record information without the help of a credit repair organization and that you have a right to order a copy of your credit record from a credit bureau. It must also highlight your rights when you hire a credit repair organization, including the right to sue the organization for violating the CROA.

- Cannot make misleading statements to you, provide you with misleading advice, or attempt to deceive you in any way.

- Cannot encourage you to alter your identity in order to build a new, problem-free credit history for yourself.

The Electronic Fund Transfer Act

The Electronic Fund Transfer Act (EFTA) applies to Automated Teller Machines (ATMs), debit cards, direct deposits, pay-by-phone systems (that let you call your financial institution with instructions to pay certain bills or to transfer funds from one of your accounts to another), personal computing banking, and electronic check conversions. (These conversions change a paper check into an electronic payment.)

The law requires financial institutions to inform you of your electronic fund transfer (EFT) rights and responsibilities before you contract for EFT services or make your first electronic transfer. Among other things, the laws says that a financial institution must provide you with the following information:

- A summary of your liability resulting from unauthorized transfers due to the loss or theft of your ATM or debit card, or your PIN.

- The telephone number and address of who to notify if you think an unauthorized transfer has been or may be made, as well as a statement of the institution's business days (generally, the days it is open to the public for regular business), and the number of days you have to report suspected unauthorized transfers.

- The phone number you should call to report a loss or theft or to report an unauthorized transfer.

- A description of its error resolution procedure.

- The type of transfers you can make, associated transfer fees, and any limits on the frequency and dollar amount of the transfers.

- A summary of your right to receive documentation of your transfers, to stop payment on a pre-authorized transfer, and the procedures you must use to stop payment.

- A description of the procedure you must follow to report an error on one of your EFT receipts or on your periodic statement, to request more information about a transfer listed on the statement, and information regarding how long you have to report an error.

- A summary of the institution's liability to you if it fails to make or stop certain transactions.

- A description of when the institution will disclose information about your account to third parties.

- A notice that you may be charged a fee if you use an ATM where you don't have an account.

- Your right to receive written records related to your electronic fund transfers.

- Information about how to stop payment on a pre-authorized transfer.

The EFTA also requires financial institutions to give you advance notice of any change in your account that will increase your costs or liability, or limit your transfers, although there are exceptions. The law also entitles you to a quarterly statement regardless of whether or not you made any electronic transfers during that quarter and a periodic statement for each statement cycle in which you make an electronic transfer. That statement must indicate the amount of a transfer, the date it was credited or debited to your account, the type of transfer and type of account(s) to or from which funds were transferred, and which address and telephone number to use if you have an inquiry about the transfer.

The EFTA forbids creditors from requiring you to repay a loan or other credit that you owe to them using an electronic fund transfer except in the case of an overdraft checking account.

Resolving errors: If you find an error in one of your EFT account statements, the EFTA requires you to notify your bank within 60 days of receiving the first statement that contains the error. Although the law says that you can call or write the financial institution, it's best to write. In your letter, include your account number, your name, explain what you think the problem is, the dollar amount involved, and the date of the error. If you call instead of write, the bank may ask you to send this same information in writing within 10 business days. Send your letter certified mail and request a return receipt.

 Warning If you don't notify the financial institution within 60 days about a problem in your EFT account statement, it is under no obligation to conduct an investigation.

After the financial institution receives your phone call or letter, it must conduct an investigation into your problem within 10 days and must report the results of its investigation within three business days of completing it. However, if the financial institution needs more time to complete its investigation, the financial institution can have up to 45 additional days, assuming the money in dispute is returned to your account and you're notified promptly of the credit. If the alleged error involves an account that you opened during the past 30 days, the financial institution can take up to 90 days to investigate your problem and can have up to 20 business days to credit your account if it finds that there is an error in your account.

If the financial institution finds an error in your EFT account statement, it must correct the error within one business day. If it does not find an error, it may take the money back assuming it sends you a written explanation.

The law also says that if you find an error in your bank statement related to a point-of-sale purchase that you made with your debit card, you should contact the card issuer at the address or phone number it provides for addressing such problems. Once you've notified the company about the error, it has 10 business days to investigate and to report its findings to you, although in certain circumstances, it can have up to 90 days to complete the investigation. Once its investigation is over, the financial institution must notify you of its findings. If it found that your statement is in error, the financial institution must correct the problem right away. If it concludes that your bank statement is accurate, it must send you a written notice explaining why and let you know that it deducted from your account any money that it may have recredited to the account during its investigation. You are entitled to ask the financial institution to provide you with copies of any documents it relied on during its investigation.

Lost or stolen ATM and debit cards and PINS: The EFTA also applies to lost or stolen ATM and debit cards and PINs. If you report a loss or theft to the card issuer before someone

204

uses it without your permission, you will not be responsible for any unauthorized withdrawals. If you report it within two days of the loss or theft, you can only be held liable for $50 worth of unauthorized charges. However, if you wait until the third day to report it, your potential liability jumps to $500. And, if you don't report it for at least 60 days, you may lose the entire balance in your account plus your maximum overdraft line of credit, if any. However, if there is an extenuating reason why you did not notify the financial institution right away of the loss or theft, if you were very ill for example, the financial institution must give you a reasonable amount of additional time to report the loss or theft of your ATM or debit card or of your PIN.

Once you report the loss or theft, you will not be responsible for any additional unauthorized transfers that may occur after that time. If you find any on your statements, contact the financial institution right away using the procedures it has established for reporting errors.

Warning   Under most circumstances, if you use an electronic fund transfer to purchase something, the EFTA does not give you the right to stop payment should your purchase turn out to be defective or if is never delivered. However, you can stop payment when you've arranged for your account to be regularly debited in order to pay a third party like your insurance company, health club, and so on, assuming you notify your financial institution at least three business days before the transfer is scheduled to occur.

What to Do If You Think That Your Legal Rights Have Been Violated

There are several actions that you can take if you believe that your federal legal rights have been violated. You can:

- Write a letter of complaint to the business that you believe has committed the violation.
- File a lawsuit.
- Complain to the appropriate government agency.

The rest of this chapter discusses each of these alternatives.

Write a Complaint Letter

Writing a polite letter of complaint is usually a good starting place when you believe that your legal rights have been violated. This is because the violation may be the result of an innocent oversight or error on the part of the business, because you may be confused about your rights, and because it costs very little to write and mail a letter and the letter may get you the results that you want. If it does not, the other alternatives are still available to you.

If the business you are having a problem with is locally owned, send your letter to its manager or owner. If the business is national, write to its consumer affairs or consumer relations manager or credit manager. If you are unsure about to whom to direct your letter, call the business and ask.

Explain in your letter how you believe that your rights have been violated—be as specific as possible—and indicate which law you believe has been violated. Also, note all applicable dates, explain what you have already done to try to resolve your problem and the outcome of your efforts and provide the names and titles of whomever you spoke with. Be sure to include your contact information, including daytime and evening phone numbers and your mailing address, so that the business can follow up with you. Attach to your letter any documentation you may have that further explains or relates to your problem—cancelled checks, copies of correspondence, and receipts, for example.

File a Lawsuit

If a friendly letter does not resolve your problem, you may want to consider scheduling an appointment with a consumer law attorney, especially if you have a lot of money at stake, a debt collector has made your life miserable, your credit history and/or credit score has been harmed by an error in your credit file, and so on. Meet with an attorney who has specific experience dealing with the particular kind of problem you are having. The next section provides resources you can use to locate a qualified attorney in your area.

The attorney you meet with will ask questions to determine the exact nature of your legal problem and to assess the strength of your case. The attorney may suggest trying to resolve your legal problem by sending the business that violated your legal rights a letter on his or her law firm's letterhead. Sometimes this letter will scare the business into taking action because it does not want to be sued. However, if the letter does not get results, the attorney may suggest that you sue the business.

If the attorney believes that you have a good basis for a lawsuit, he or she will decide whether to bring your lawsuit in state or federal court, assuming your state has a law that applies to your problem. The attorney will also determine how much you can sue for and what kinds of information he or she will need in order to build a winnable case for you. If you don't have the information the attorney needs, even if your rights have been violated, you may not have a strong case and the attorney may not want to represent you. This is why it is so important when you are having a problem with a creditor or some other business to document the problem, make copies of all letters you send and receive related to the problem, hold on to receipts, keep a record of your phone conversations related to the problem, and so on.

When your case is strong, the attorney will probably agree to represent you on a contingent fee basis, which means that you won't have to pay the attorney any money up-front and that if you win, the attorney will get paid by taking a percentage of the money that you are awarded by the court. The court may also order the business to pay your attorney's expenses and court costs. If you lose your lawsuit, all you will probably owe the attorney is the amount of his or her expenses and court costs. How much you owe will depend on the terms of your agreement with the attorney.

If you can't find an attorney willing to take your case on a contingent fee basis, you should take that fact as an indication that you do not have a strong basis for a lawsuit and you should probably drop your plans to sue.

Resources for locating a consumer law attorney: You can use these resources to find a qualified attorney who can help you with legal problems relating to getting and using credit, spending money, dealing with debt collectors, resolving problems related to your credit history or to credit reporting agencies, as well as problems with credit repair organizations. Remember, however, a referral from one of the resources on this list is not the same as an endorsement. Therefore, you should meet with an attorney first to determine for yourself if you believe that he or she is someone you will feel comfortable working with, to discuss how the attorney proposes dealing with your legal problem and to find out how the attorney will charge you for his or her services. By the way, your initial meeting with the attorney should be free, but confirm that fact by asking when you call to schedule an appointment.

Resources that can help you find an attorney include:

- A friend or relative who had a problem similar to yours and who was happy with their attorney
- Your local or state bar association
- The National Consumer Law Center at (617) 542-8010 or at www.consumerlaw.org
- The National Association of Consumer Advocates (NACA) at (202) 452-1989 or at www.naca.net

Complain to a Government Agency

If a friendly letter does not accomplish your goal, it's a good idea to file a formal complaint against the business with the appropriate federal agency. This is advisable even if you decide to sue the business. Although these agencies will not resolve your particular problem, it may take action against the business you complain about if it receives enough consumer complaints about the business to establish a pattern of illegal behavior. Also, it may take action against an entire class of businesses if it determines that the problem you complain about is prevalent within the business's industry.

If your state has a law that applies to your legal problem, write a complaint letter to the appropriate state as well as federal agency. Check with the consumer protection office of your state attorney general's office to find out about the consumer laws in your state.

Which agency to contact: The specific federal agency to contact about your complaint depends on the nature of your legal problem and the type of business with whom you have a complaint. For example, the Federal Trade Commission (FTC) is charged with enforcing laws related to most creditors, as well as laws relating to credit reporting agencies, credit repair firms, and debt collectors, among others. The FTC's contact information is:

Federal Trade Commission
Consumer Response Center
600 Pennsylvania Ave., NW
Washington, DC 20580
(800) 382-4357
www.ftc.gov

If your complaint concerns a federally chartered or federally insured savings and loan association, write to:

Office of Thrift Supervision
Compliance PolicyDepartment of the Treasury
1700 G St., NW
Washington, DC 20552
(877) 382-4357
www.ots.treas.gov

If you want to complain about a state-chartered bank that is insured by the Federal Deposit Insurance Corporation but is not a member of the Federal Reserve System, you should write to:

Federal Deposit Insurance Corporation (FDIC)
Consumer Affairs Branch
Compliance and Consumer Affairs Division
Supervision and Consumer Protection Division
550 17th St., NW
Washington, DC 20429
(877) 275-3342
www2.fdic.gov/starsmail/index.html (e-mail)
www.fdic.gov/consumers/index.html (web site)

If your complaint is with a state-chartered bank or trust company that is a member of the Federal Reserve System, contact:

Federal Reserve Consumer Help
PO Box 1200
Minneapolis, MN 55480
(888) 851-1920
(877) 766-8533 (TDD)
(877) 888-2520 (fax)
ConsumerHelp@FederalReserve.gov
www.federalreserve.gov

If your complaint is with a nationally chartered bank (National or N.A. will be part of its name), contact:

Comptroller of the Currency
Customer Assistance Group
1301 McKinney Street
Suite 3450
Houston, TX 77010
www.occ.treas.gov/customer.htm

If your complaint concerns a federally chartered credit union, write to:

National Credit Union Administration
Consumer Affairs Division
1775 Duke Street
Alexandria, VA 22314
(703) 518-6300
www.ncua.gov/ConsumerInformation

Budgeting Worksheet

Monthly Income	Current Income	Revised Income
Your take-home pay	$_____	$_____
Your spouse's/partner's take-home pay	$_____	$_____
Alimony	$_____	$_____
Child support	$_____	$_____
Other income (type)	$_____	$_____
TOTAL MONTHLY INCOME	$_____	$_____

Monthly Expenses	Current Payments	Revised Expenses
FIXED EXPENSES		
Mortgage	$_____	$_____
Rent	$_____	$_____
Car loan (or car lease)	$_____	$_____
Home equity loan	$_____	$_____
Other loans	$_____	$_____
Credit cards	$_____	$_____

Monthly Expenses	Current Payments	Revised Expenses
FIXED EXPENSES *(continued)*		
Child care	$_____	$_____
After school activities	$_____	$_____
Children's allowances	$_____	$_____
Child support	$_____	$_____
Alimony	$_____	$_____
Dues	$_____	$_____
Insurance		
Home owner/renter	$_____	$_____
Car	$_____	$_____
Health	$_____	$_____
Life	$_____	$_____
Other insurance	$_____	$_____
Other fixed expenses	$_____	$_____
VARIABLE EXPENSES		
Electricity and water	$_____	$_____
Gas/oil	$_____	$_____
Gasoline for car	$_____	$_____
Parking	$_____	$_____
Tolls	$_____	$_____
Public transportation	$_____	$_____
Groceries	$_____	$_____
Alcohol	$_____	$_____
Cigarettes	$_____	$_____
Cleaning supplies	$_____	$_____
Toiletries	$_____	$_____
Haircuts and other self care	$_____	$_____

Appendix A

Monthly Expenses	Current Payments	Revised Expenses
VARIABLE EXPENSES *(continued)*		
Phone service	$_____	$_____
Cell phone	$_____	$_____
Cable	$_____	$_____
Internet service	$_____	$_____
Out-of-pocket medical expenses	$_____	$_____
Home repairs and maintenance	$_____	$_____
Clothes	$_____	$_____
Dry cleaning	$_____	$_____
Entertainment		
Video rental	$_____	$_____
Movies	$_____	$_____
Concerts	$_____	$_____
Sporting activities/events	$_____	$_____
Dining out	$_____	$_____
Other	$_____	$_____
Books, magazines, and newspapers	$_____	$_____
Allowances	$_____	$_____
Gifts	$_____	$_____
Charitable donations	$_____	$_____
Other variable expenses	$_____	$_____
PERIODIC EXPENSES		
Property taxes	$_____	$_____
Tuition	$_____	$_____
Auto registration and license	$_____	$_____
Other periodic expenses	$_____	$_____
TOTAL EXPENSES	$_____	$_____

(continued)

Monthly Expenses	Current Payments	Revised Expenses
CONTRIBUTIONS TO SAVINGS, RETIREMENT, AND INVESTMENTS		
Savings account	$_____	$_____
Contributions to retirement plan	$_____	$_____
Investments (stocks, mutual funds, etc.)	$_____	$_____
TOTAL EXPENSES AND CONTRIBUTIONS	$_____	$_____
TOTAL NET MONTHLY INCOME	$_____	$_____
SUBTRACT YOUR MONTHLY INCOME FROM YOUR EXPENSES AND CONTRIBUTIONS	$_____	$_____
NET SURPLUS OR DEFICIT	$_____	$_____

Appendix B

Your Household Budget

Monthly Income	Amount Budgeted
Your take-home pay	$_____
Your spouse or partner's take-home pay	$_____
Alimony	$_____
Child support	$_____
Other income (type)	$_____
TOTAL MONTHLY INCOME	$_____

Monthly Expenses	Amount Budgeted
FIXED EXPENSES	
Mortgage or rent	$_____
Car loan (or car lease)	$_____
Home equity loan	$_____
Other loans	$_____
Credit cards	$_____
Child care	$_____
After-school activities	$_____
Children's allowances	$_____

(continued)

Monthly Expenses		Amount Budgeted
FIXED EXPENSES *(continued)*		
Child support		$_____
Alimony		$_____
Dues		$_____
Insurance		
Home owner/renter	$_____	
Car	$_____	
Health	$_____	
Life	$_____	
Other insurance	$_____	
Total insurance		$_____
Other fixed expenses		$_____
VARIABLE EXPENSES		
Electricity and water		$_____
Gas/Oil		$_____
Gasoline for car		$_____
Parking		$_____
Tolls		$_____
Public transportation		$_____
Groceries		$_____
Alcohol		$_____
Cigarettes		$_____
Cleaning supplies		$_____
Toiletries		$_____
Haircuts and other self care		$_____
Phone service		$_____
Cell phone		$_____
Cable		$_____

(continued)

Monthly Expenses		Amount Budgeted
VARIABLE EXPENSES *(continued)*		
Internet service		$_____
Out-of-pocket medical expenses		$_____
Home repairs and maintenance		$_____
Clothes		$_____
Dry cleaning		$_____
Entertainment		
Video rental	$_____	
Movies	$_____	
Concerts	$_____	
Sporting activities/events	$_____	
Dining out	$_____	
Other	$_____	
Total entertainment		$_____
Books, magazines, and newspapers		$_____
Allowances		$_____
Gifts		$_____
Charitable donations		$_____
Other variable expenses		$_____
PERIODIC EXPENSES		
Property taxes		$_____
Tuition		$_____
Auto registration and license		$_____
Other periodic expenses		$_____
TOTAL EXPENSES		$_____

(continued)

Appendix B

Monthly Expenses	Amount Budgeted
CONTRIBUTIONS TO SAVINGS, RETIREMENT AND INVESTMENTS	
Savings account	$
Contributions to retirement plan	$
CONTRIBUTIONS TO SAVINGS, RETIREMENT AND INVESTMENTS	
Investments (stocks, mutual funds, etc.)	$
TOTAL EXPENSES AND CONTRIBUTIONS	$
TOTAL NET MONTHLY INCOME	$
TOTAL MONTHLY INCOME AND CONTRIBUTIONS	$
NET SURPLUS (DEFICIT)	$

Appendix C

Helpful Resources

This Appendix lists government agencies, nonprofit organizations, web sites, and books that can help you deal with your debts and manage your finances responsibly.

Organizations and Web Sites

American Bankruptcy Institute (ABI)

You can find a lot of good information about managing your debt and bankruptcy in the *Consumer Corner* section of the ABI's web site, www.abiworld.org/consumer. If you decide that filing for bankruptcy is your best option, you can locate a board-certified bankruptcy attorney in your area at this site as well.

Bankrate.com

You'll find plenty of practical advice about managing your finances, using credit, choosing a bankcard, handling your debt, and more at this web site, www.bankrate.com. Sign up for Bankrate.com's free newsletter, which provides news and other information that can help you manage your finances wisely.

Better Business Bureau (BBB)

The BBB is a national nonprofit organization that promotes honest, ethical practices among businesses. Local BBBs also maintain information regarding whether or not there are any unanswered or unsettled consumer complaints claims against a local business, and help consumers resolve problems with their business members. For more information about the BBB, call your local organization or get in touch with its national office at (703) 276-0100. You can also visit the BBB's web site at www.bbb.org.

Cardratings.com

Use this site as a resource for helping you find a good credit card and for comparing card offers, www.cardratings.com.

Consolidated Credit Counseling Services, Inc. (Consolidated Credit)

A national organization that assists consumers throughout the United States resolve their financial problems through education and professional counseling. It also offers consumers the opportunity to participate in its debt management program. For more information, call

(800) SAVE-ME-2 (800-728-3632) or visit Consolidated Credit's web site at www.consolidatedcredit.org.

Debtors Anonymous (DA)

If you believe that you are addicted to spending, this organization can help if you are ready to overcome your problem. It uses the same time-proven techniques as Alcoholics Anonymous. You can locate the nearest DA chapter by going to the organization's web site at www.debtorsanonymous.org, or by calling (781) 452-2743.

Debtsmart's E-mail Newsletter

This free newsletter provides information about ways to save money, how to budget, and so on. To read the newsletter, go to www.debtsmart.com.

Federal Consumer Action Web Site

This web site, www.consumeraction.org is part of the Federal Citizen Information Center. It offers a wealth of information about shopping for consumer goods and services, how to avoid problems and how to resolve them if problems develop. It also provides an invaluable directory of consumer organizations, trade groups, associations, corporations, and government agencies to contact when you are having a consumer problem. Many of the organizations in the directory have dispute resolution programs. For a hard copy of the information at the Consumer Action web site, call (888) 878-3256. Ask for a copy of the *Consumer Action Handbook* or go to www.pueblo.gsa.gov.

Federal Trade Commission (FTC)

This regulatory agency works to protect consumers from fraudulent, deceptive, and unfair business practices and provides consumers with information to help educate them about their legal rights. Go to the FTC's web site at www.ftc.gov to file a complaint against a business or organization and to read a wide variety of informative brochures and fact sheets. You can also order those publications at the web site.

National Consumer Law Center (NCLC)

If you have a low income and need help dealing with a debt collection problem, foreclosure, repossession, loss of utility service, and so on, this national organization can help. To find a NCLC consumer law attorney in your area, go to www.consumerlaw.org or call (617) 542-8010.

Books

After Bankruptcy: Simple Steps to Rebuilding Your Credit and Your Life, Anne Whiteley, Toronto, Ontario: Solstice Publishing, 2001.

The Bankruptcy Kit, 3rd edition, John Ventura, Chicago: Dearborn Trade Publishing, 2004.

Bounce Back from Bankruptcy: A Step-by-Step Guide to Getting Back on Your Financial Feet, Paula Langguth Ryan, Pellingham, Victoria, BC: Casper Communications, 2001.

The Budget Kit, 4th edition, Judy Lawrence, Chicago: Dearborn Trade Publishing, 2004.

Cheap Talk with Frugal Friends: Over 600 Tips, Tricks and Creative Ideas for Saving Money, Angie Zalwski, Deana Ricks, Lancaster, PA: Starburst Publishers, 2001.

The Complete Cheapskate: How to Get Out of Debt, Stay Out and Break Free From Money Worries Forever, Mary Hart, New York: St. Martin's Press, 2003.

Debt-Free By 30: Practical Advice for the Young, Broke & Upwardly Mobile, Jason Anthony and Karl Cluck, New York: Plume, 2001.

50 Simple Things You Can Do to Improve Your Finances: How to Spend Less, Save More and Make the Most of What You Have, Ilyce Glink, New York: Three Rivers Press, 2001.

Frugal Friends: Making the Most of Your Hard Earned Money, Jonni McCoy, Yonkers, NY: Dimensions, 2003.

Frugal Living for Dummies, Deborah Taylor-Hough, New York: John Wiley & Sons, 2003.

Good Advice for a Bad Economy, John Ventura and Mary Reed, New York: Berkley Books, 2003.

How to Save Money Every Day, Ellie Kay, Washington, DC: Bethany House, 2001.

Money Troubles, 5th Edition, Robin Leonard, Berkeley, CA: Nolo Press, 1997.

Stop Debt Collectors Cold, John Ventura, Gerri Detweiler, and Mary Reed. To order go to www.stopdebtcollectorscold .com.

The Ultimate Credit Handbook, 3rd edition, Gerri Detweiler, New York: Plume, 2003.

Appendix D

About Consolidated Credit Counseling Services, Inc.

Consolidated Credit Counseling Services, Inc. (Consolidated Credit) is an organization whose mission is to assist consumers throughout the United States resolve their financial problems through education and professional counseling. It also offers consumers the opportunity to participate in its debt management program.

Founded in the early 1990s, the organization has a friendly, service-oriented staff of trained professionals who are dedicated to helping consumers solve their money management and debt problems. These professionals counsel a wide range of financially troubled consumers, from the unemployed to individuals who are earning well over $100,000 a year.

Resolving Your Debt Problems through the Consolidated's Debt Management Program

The Consolidated Credit Debt Management Program helps consumers when they have too much unsecured debt, including credit card debts. The program helps them consolidate their debts and lower their monthly debt payments. Usually, this is done by negotiating lower interest rates with the consumers' creditors and getting late and over-limit fees waived. Most consumers who participate in the Consolidated Credit Debt Management Program will reduce their payments by 30 to 50 percent and reduce or even eliminate interest charges as well as late and over limit fees, which may translate into savings of hundreds, maybe thousands of dollars.

If you decide to enroll in the program, a professionally trained and certified counselor will analyze your financial situation and then contact your unsecured creditors to negotiate with them. Once the details of your debt management plan have been worked out, you will be responsible for paying a set amount of money each month to a special Consolidated Credit surety and trust account. Consolidated Credit will use those funds to pay the participating creditors. As proof that your payments were made, you will continue to receive monthly account statements from those creditors.

Tip

You must close any accounts that are included in your debt management plan and you cannot open any new credit accounts until you have completed the plan. Additionally, any insurance coverage purchased through the accounts must be cancelled.

For more information about Consolidated Credit and its Debt Management Program, call 800-SAVE-ME-2 (800-728-3632). You can also visit the organization's web site at www.consolidatedcredit.org.

The Benefits of Participating in the Debt Management Program

There are many important benefits to participating in the Consolidated Credit Debt Management Program. For example:

- You will lower your unsecured debt payments.

- The amount of interest and penalties you owe will be reduced or even eliminated. That means that more of your monthly payments will go toward paying down your debt principal and potentially, you will save thousands of dollars and years of payments.

- Rather than having to make payments to many unsecured creditors and worrying about paying them all on time, you will only have to make one payment each month to pay off those debts.

- Your credit record and credit score should improve. Consolidated Credit will attempt to re-age all of your past due accounts so that they will show up in your credit history as current.

- You will get out of debt faster. Most participants in the Consolidated Credit Debt Management Program get rid of their unsecured debts in three to five years.

- You avoid bankruptcy. Participating in the program decreases the likelihood that you will damage your credit history even more than it already is by having to file for bankruptcy.

- You put an end to the financial stress in your life. Knowing that you are working with a team of professionals who are committed to helping you resolve your financial troubles will make you worry less about your debts and feel more hopeful about your financial future.

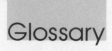

Glossary

I n this glossary, you will find definitions for commonly used terms related to credit and debt. Knowing what these terms mean will help you make more informed decisions about your finances.

Acceleration Clause   A provision in a loan agreement that allows a creditor to demand payment in full when you do not meet the terms of the agreement.

Accrued Interest   Interest that accumulates over time on a debt that you owe.

Annual Percentage Rate (APR)   The cost of credit, expressed as a yearly rate. The Federal Truth in Lending Act requires that all offers for credit indicate the credit's APR so that consumers can understand the cost of the credit they are applying for and so they can compare credit offers.

Balloon Payment   A final payment on a loan that is substantially larger than previous payments.

Bankruptcy   A legal procedure governed by federal law that helps consumers who have too much debt. There are two bankruptcy options for consumers—Chapter 13 reorganization and Chapter 11 liquidation. If you file for Chapter 13, you will have three to five years to pay off your debts and the balance of what you owe on certain debts will be wiped out at the end of that time. Some debts will remain. If you file for Chapter 11, you will have to give up certain assets so that they can be sold and the proceeds will be applied to your debts.

Cash Advance   Cash obtained from a credit card.

Cash Value   The savings portion of a whole life, universal, or variable life insurance policy. You can borrow against that value.

Closed-End Credit   A loan that you must repay by making fixed payments over a specified period of time.

Collection Agency   A business that collects past due debts for other businesses, as well as individuals. Most collection agencies get paid for their services by taking a percentage of what they collect for their clients.

Collateral   Assets pledged as security for a secured debt. If you do not pay a debt that you have collateralized, the creditor can take the collateral.

Cosigner   Someone who signs a credit agreement so that if the main borrower does not repay the debt according to the terms of the agreement, the creditor can look to that other person for payment. The main borrower and the cosigner are equally responsible for the debt.

Credit Agreement   A contract between a borrower and a creditor that details the amount borrowed, the applicable interest rate and all other terms of the credit.

Credit Bureau   A business that gathers information regarding a consumer's use of credit and provides that information to businesses and organizations legally authorized to review it. Also called a credit reporting agency.

Credit History   A record of how you have managed your credit over time that is maintained by a credit bureau. Creditors, insurers, employers, and landlords use consumer credit record information as well as credit scores based on that information to make decisions about consumers. Also called a credit record, credit report, or credit file.

Credit Insurance   Repays a loan in the event of your death or disability.

Credit Practices Rule   Protects you when you apply for credit with a retail business, auto dealer, credit union, or finance company by requiring that they include specific disclosures in their consumer credit contracts. The disclosures relate to your rights should you fail to repay the credit according to the contract's terms. It also requires that you be provided with certain written information if you agree to cosign someone else's credit and gives you specific rights when it comes to late fees.

Credit Repair   The process of removing inaccurate or outdated information from a credit record. Some credit repair firms use illegal methods to remove negative but accurate information from a consumer's credit file.

Credit Repair Organizations Act   A federal law that regulates the activities of credit repair organizations and that gives consumers specific rights when they work with such an organization.

Credit Score A number that is derived from the information in your credit history and that is an indicator how well you are likely to manage credit in the future.

Creditor A person or business to whom you owe money.

Debit Card Allows you to pay for purchases out of your bank account or money market account without writing a check. The money for the purchase may come directly out of your account at the time of purchase or your account may be debited for the cost of the transaction a couple days later if you use the card like a charge card.

Debt Consolidation The process of taking out a larger loan to pay off one or more smaller loans.

Default What you do when you do not live up to the terms of a credit agreement.

Default Judgment A court judgment issued by a judge when you are sued and don't respond to the lawsuit.

Deficiency The difference between what you owe on a secured debt and what the asset that secures it sells for.

Discharge What happens when the court erases certain debts at the end of your bankruptcy so that you will not have to pay them.

Down Payment The initial amount of money you may have to pay when you make a credit purchase. For example, you make a down payment on a home. The down payment reduces the amount that you must finance and helps protects the lender should you default on your credit agreement.

Electronic Funds Transfer Act A federal law that provides you with limited protections when unauthorized purchases and withdrawals are made using your ATM or debit card or when errors related to purchases and withdrawals you made with your ATM or debit card appear on your bank statement.

Equal Credit Opportunity Act A federal act that prohibits creditors from discriminating against you during the credit application process on the basis of your race, religion, national origin, sex, age, or marital status, or because you receive public assistance. It also requires creditors to respond to your credit application within 30 days of receiving it. If you are denied credit or granted less credit than you applied for, the law requires that the creditor give you a specific reason for the denial.

Equity The difference between what your home is worth and the balance due on your mortgage and on any other financial obligations that your home may secure.

Exempt Assets The assets you are allowed to keep if a creditor gets a legal judgment against you because you have not paid a debt or if you file for bankruptcy. Every state has a law that spells out the types of assets consumers can claim as exempt. Additionally, there are federal exemptions that consumers can use in bankruptcy.

Fair Credit Billing Act A federal act that establishes procedures for correcting billing errors when you purchase a product or service using a credit card or retail store charge card. Under this law, you are protected if someone you did not authorize uses your credit card or retail store charge.

The law also protects you when you purchase merchandise with a credit card or retail store charge card and turns out to be defective, damaged, shoddily made, or not delivered. Furthermore, if you pay for a service with your credit card or retail store charge and the service is not delivered or not provided according to the terms of your contract.

Fair Credit and Charge Card Disclosure Act Part of the Federal Truth in Lending Act, this law requires creditors to provide you with specific information when you apply for credit or when they send you an offer for credit. The information tells you how much the credit will cost you to use and it helps you compare credit offers so you know which one has the best terms.

Fair Credit Reporting Act A federal act that gives consumers specific rights when it comes to the information in their credit histories. It also establishes specific responsibilities for credit bureaus, suppliers of information to credit bureaus and users of that information.

Fair Debt Collection Practices Act A federal law that regulates the activities of debt collectors and establishes your rights when you are contacted by a debt collector.

Finance Charge Another term for the amount of interest you pay a credit card company when you do not pay your card balance in full each month as well as the amount of interest you pay on your outstanding loan balance. The finance charge is expressed as a percentage rate, for example, 3.9 percent, 9.9 percent, 19 percent, or some other amount.

Forbearance When a creditor agrees not to collect on a debt.

Foreclosure The process whereby a mortgage lender or another creditor with a lien on your home or on some other piece of real estate that you own takes that asset because you did not live up to the terms of your agreement with the creditor.

Grace Period The time during which you can pay your account balance in full without incurring a finance charge.

Home Equity Line of Credit A type of credit that allows you to tap the equity in your home as needed up to a certain dollar amount. Your home serves as collateral.

Home Equity Loan Consumer Protection Act A federal law that requires a creditor to provide you with certain information when you apply for a home equity line of credit so that you can understand the true cost of the credit and can compare it to similar offers.

Identity Theft and Assumption Deterrence Act This federal law makes stealing your identity a criminal act and establishes your rights when you are the victim of identity fraud.

Installment Loan A loan that you repay over time by making periodic payments of principle and interest at specific intervals.

Judgment The court's final decision at the end of a lawsuit.

Judgment Proof When you have no assets that a creditor can take in order to satisfy a judgment against you.

Lien A creditor's claim against property you own. When a creditor has a lien on one of your assets, if you do not pay the debt that is associated with that lien, the creditor has a legal right to take the property. Your mortgage lender has a lien against your home and your car lender has a lien on your car.

Mortgage Loan A loan to purchase real estate. The loan is secured by the real estate.

Open-End Credit Agreement A credit agreement with no specific date by which you must pay the account balance in full although you must make monthly minimum payments on the balance. Credit cards are a common example of open-ended credit as are retail store charge cards and gasoline cards.

Periodic Rate An interest rate that changes periodically. The terms of the change are spelled out in your credit agreement.

Personal Property An asset that can be moved, as opposed to real estate, which is fixed. Your personal property may include vehicles, furniture, jewelry, fine art, and so on.

Prepayment Penalty A penalty you may apply if you pay off a loan early. The penalty helps compensate the lender for the fact that it will not earn as much interest income on the loan as if you had continued paying on it until the loan term was up.

Principal The amount of money you borrow. Principal does not include interest.

Punitive Damages Money that a court may order a business to pay you as punishment for harming you in some way and to encourage the business not to repeat its illegal behavior.

Refinance To pay off an existing loan and get a new loan in order to lower your interest rate, get more or less time to pay off the original loan, and so on. You may also refinance as a way to raise cash and liquidate equity.

Repossession When a secured creditor takes back your collateral—your car, for example—because you did not live up to your agreement with the creditor.

Secured Credit Card A credit card that is secured by money in your savings account or by a Certificate of Deposit. You can only borrow up to a percentage of the money in the account or the value of your Certificate of Deposit. If you do not pay on your credit card according to the terms of your credit agreement, the creditor can take the funds in your savings account or your Certificate of Deposit.

Secured Creditor A creditor that has a lien on one of your assets. If you do not pay the creditor according to the terms of your agreement with one another, the creditor is entitled to take the asset, also referred to as collateral.

Secured Debt A debt that you collateralized with an asset that you own. If you do not meet the terms of your credit agreement, the lender can take that asset in lieu of payment. Common examples of secured debts include car loans and mortgages.

Security Agreement An agreement associated with a secured loan. The agreement specifies the collateral that secures the loan and under what circumstances the creditor can take the collateral, among other things. Notice of the existence of a security agreement is sometimes filed with your local courthouse as evidence of the lien.

Term   The length of time that a loan agreement will be in effect—from the date that the agreement is signed to the date that the loan will be paid in full.

Truth in Lending Act   A federal law that requires specific disclosures about the terms of credit so that consumers can make informed decisions regarding whether a particular credit offer is a good deal for them. It also gives you a variety of other rights when you apply for or use credit.

Unsecured Debt   A debt for which no assets are pledged to guarantee payment. The most common type of unsecured debt is credit card debt.

Usury Laws   State laws that regulate the interest rates that creditors can charge consumers.

Wage Garnishment   What may happen if you do not pay a debt that you owe. The creditor you owe the money to could get a judgment against you and then get the court's permission to take a percentage of your wages in order to get its money. Your employer will be legally required to deduct the garnishment amount from your paychecks. Not all states permit wage garnishment.

About the Author

Howard S. Dvorkin is a certified public accountant, a certified credit counselor, and a nationally known expert on consumer credit and debt issues. As the founder of Consolidated Credit Counseling Services, Inc., a national nonprofit agency, he is a leader in the debt-counseling field and has helped millions of families resolve their money problems.

As an expert on consumer credit trends and the causes and effects of being financially over-extended, Dvorkin has been interviewed by the *Wall Street Journal*, the *New York Times*, *Chicago Tribune*, *Fortune*, *USA Today*, *Entrepreneur*, the *American Banker*, *Investor's Business Daily*, as well as a host of national and local newspapers around the country and web sites such as CBS MarketWatch.com, Bankrate.com, and CNNfn.com. He has also been a guest on countless national and local television and radio programs, including the *ABC World News*, *CBS Nightly News*, *The Early Show*, FOX News, and CNN.

Dvorkin consults with many organizations regarding proper operational procedures, educational marketing, and industry trends. He has been instrumental in the growth of the Association of Independent Consumer Credit Counseling Agencies (AICCCA), a national trade association for the consumer credit industry. He is the past president of the AICCCA and has held positions as the vice president, and chairman of the Client Retention Committee. He is dedicated to public outreach initiatives and has contributed his time, knowledge, and resources to educating consumers about personal finance. He has helped thousands of individuals face and conquer devastating financial hardships and avoid personal bankruptcy.

Mr. Dvorkin was awarded the South Florida 2007 Diamond Award. The award acknowledges outstanding individuals who exhibit exceptional leadership, who have helped set standards in the corporate community, and who have improved the quality of life for South Florida businesses and residents. In 2006, Mr. Dvorkin was honored at the annual gala for the State of Israel Bonds and awarded the Israel Bonds Commemorative Medallion for his good works for the betterment of the State of Israel. He was the *South Florida Business Journal*'s Nonprofit Heavy Hitter in 2005. This award is presented to outstanding individuals for their contribution to nonprofit organizations in South Florida. He was also twice nominated for the Ernst & Young Entrepreneur of the Year Award in 2004 and 2006 and has been a finalist for the *South Florida Business Journal*'s Up and Comers Award in 2002 and 2003.

With Mr. Dvorkin's guidance, Consolidated Credit Counseling Services, Inc., was selected from over 150 organizations and was chosen as the Overall Winner for the *South Florida Business Journal*'s 2006 Best Places to Work Award as well as winning the 2006 Best Places to Work, Medium-Sized Business Category. Consolidated Credit also won the 2003 Business of the Year Award, Nonprofit Category.

Mr. Dvorkin is very active in his community and has sat for over a decade on the board of directors of the Better Business Bureau of Southeast Florida. He is also a founding member of the South Florida American Heart Association board of directors, a board member of the South Florida chapter of Junior Achievement and Henderson Mental Health Centers. Mr. Dvorkin is on the board of governors of the H. Wayne Huizenga School of Business and Entrepreneurship at Nova Southeastern University. He also dedicates his time to the National Leadership Council at American University and sat on the University's Kogod School of Business board. The Kogod School of Business has inducted Mr. Dvorkin into the 1923 Society.

Mr. Dvorkin has been a guest teacher in Entrepreneurship and Management class at the American Intercontinental University as well as taught personal finance to Head Start participants. Dvorkin graduated from the University of Miami with a masters degree in Business Administration and he received his bachelor of science degree in Accounting from the American University. He is also listed in the *Marquis Who's Who in the Finance Industry*.

Index

Index